BEYOND

BUGGIES

AND

BONNETS

Brenda Nixon

All Bible references are from the King James Version.
Excerpt from *Thirty-One Days of Praise: Enjoying God Anew* by Ruth Myers, copyright © 1994, 1996, 1997, 2003 by Ruth Myers and Warren Myers. Used by permission of WaterBrook Multnomah, an imprint of the Crown Publishing Group, a division of Penguin Random House LLC. All rights reserved.
Any third party use of this material, outside of this publication, is prohibited. Interested parties must apply directly to Penguin Random House LLC for permission.
Cover Design: Bob Ousnamer

Published by EA Books, Inc.

Autographed copies may be ordered through:
Brenda Nixon
PO Box 1302
Mount Vernon, Ohio 43050
www.BrendaNixonOnAmish.blogspot.com
www.twitter.com/BrendaNixon

ISBN: 978-1-941733-28-8

What Others Are Saying

I had a few good laughs, remembering my own experiences leaving the Amish, reading Brenda Nixon's book. This book is pretty accurate of what I also experienced.

~ Joseph Slabaugh, amishmemories.com

Author/speaker/blogger Brenda Nixon has penned an honest and challenging book about "the other side of Amish life." As one who has rescued and even "adopted" several Amish youth, Nixon can speak firsthand to this aspect of Amish life. A must-read for anyone seeking the entire truth about the Amish lifestyle.

~ Kathi Macias, www.kathimacias.com
author of 50 books including the Freedom Series

Brenda's stories of the Amish community at large, and of her own interpersonal experiences of those ex-Amish who have left this secretive sect, are as compelling as they are frightening.

~ Michele Howe, author and reviewer for Publishers
Weekly,www.michelehowe.wordpress.com

Beyond Buggies and Bonnets: Seven True Stories of Former Amish provides a close look at everyday life in the Swartzentruber and conservative Old Order Amish. Nixon's research and authentic experiences provide little known facts. With careful attention to the personal needs of ex-Amish, Nixon and her family have befriended many and helped them find their way in the foreign world of the "English." A striking and significant work!

~ Cathy Messecar, author, A Still and Quiet
Soul—Embracing Contentment

Dedication

To former Amish,

Those who felt like a misfit among their own, longed for individuality, or to
feel valued,
who were ordered about instead of guided, suspected instead of accepted,
and were courageous enough to step into the "verboten" non-Amish world.
You intercepted mine, and
taught me volumes. Thank you.
I hope you feel welcome and wanted, included, special, and
emotionally stronger, that I'm guiding your growth
as you learn and advance in our English life.
Your bravery and stamina amaze me.

To my readers,

"I was brought up to believe that the only thing worth doing was to
add to the sum of accurate information in the world."
~ Margaret Mead, cultural anthropologist

Acknowledgements

Love and gratitude to Laura, who brought the "X-men" into my life and launched this learning curve; Lynsey who brought the best son-in-law into our family; and Paul who brought a "neat and orderly" atmosphere to our home when I was consumed in writing and neglected the house.

Admiration to Sandy who generously helped me feed the ravenous appetites of "my" boys and continues to show interest in their progress. And to the gracious and giving people of Lakeholm Church of the Nazarene, pastored by Scott and Wendy, who so freely responded, prayed, and loved.

Appreciation to Brenda Joyce and Kathy for your enthusiastic interest in both my friendship and this book. To my prayer team behind the scenes Marti, Julie, Lynda, Emilie, Dianne, Karen, Michele, and Alice, *my sister*. And to my Barnabas Babes who walked with me these many years.

Respect to John, and your well-moderated Amish Q&A group, for being my fact checking resource.

Contents

Chapter 1

Mosie

He tiptoed down the darkened steps. Quietly opened his farmhouse door and slipped into the night. For two miles he ran along the shadowy country road and debated his decision. Tears welled up in his eyes as he feared being caught and stopped and the dreaded consequences if he succeeded. Eighteen-year-old Mosie, one of twelve children born into a New York Amish family, fled from his familiar life and culture because "there had to be more." Wearing his hand stitched, plain clothes, and with a secreted fifty dollars tucked into his pocket, he made his stealth escape. "I never felt so alone and so wrong," he'd later say.

Frequently checking back over his shoulder. Fearful. Mosie eventually found his English (non-Amish) neighbor's home. He used their telephone and whispered into the receiver, "Can you get me now?" Then he waited . . . alone watching his panting breath steam and vaporize into the cool night air. When a car quietly inched into the driveway, Mosie exhaled with relief and climbed inside to see his contact, David. The duo drove to Ohio. Months later, Mosie's life changed again.

***

"I've never met an Amish person," I said to my daughters. "What are these guys like?"

"They're fun mom. But they're boys," shrugged my younger Laura with a roll of her eyes. "They love western shirts, cowboy boots, country music, diesel trucks, and watching cartoons. They're strong and hardworking. One's a lumberjack now." She beamed as she named each new friend at the church where both my daughters attended. "There's Dan, Andy, Uria, David, and Mosie. And a new one, Henry."

She related their similar stories. "They left under cover of night. They didn't own a car so they ran on foot from their family farm when they thought nobody was watching."

Older daughter Lynsey chipped in to explain that those who leave may not have their birth certificate. No social security number. No job. No place to live. No suitcase. No identification whatsoever. Desperate for a new life and with vague notions of our English world they leave *everything*; family, friends, food, farm life and tools, their identity— needy and vulnerable.

I struggled to imagine the resolve of these young people. *Why run? Why at night? What motivated them to be so doggedly determined to survive?* In the years to follow, I'd get my answers.

"Anyhow," Laura continued, "They're trying to find fundraising jobs to go on our church's mission trip. She paused, then asked, "Do you want to invite them to do something? They can do anything. Then you pay what you think their work is worth."

"Sure, I'll help," I said. "We have some lawn care they can do for fundraising."

***

The dew dotted my shoes that wet spring morning in 2009 as I stood in the front yard of our home. The rumble of a diesel truck grew louder as it neared our property. I watched as the unidentified truck pulled into our driveway. Out climbed four young lads. Tight jeans. Large belt buckles. Cowboy hats atop buzzed haircuts. Western, snap-front shirts and boots. The "X-Men," as my daughters lovingly called them, had arrived at our home ready to work. I had imagined long, Dutch-boy hair, and farm clothes. After Laura introduced us to each one, I assigned the job of trimming our trees. As they busied themselves, my daughters told me more about the guys' upbringings and their sacrifices to start new lives in a world they were warned to avoid.

Quiet, reserved, industrious Mosie blended in, working intensely alongside the others. I hardly noticed him although when he spoke I detected his slight stutter and Deutch accent.

Laura told me that Mosie's parents shunned him for leaving the Amish. She explained that within months of him being on the outside they'd discovered his whereabouts, and mailed a letter telling him he wasn't welcome back even for a funeral or wedding. They believed he was turned over to Satan—going to hell—for leaving the Amish. No redemption.

Wow, I thought. *At eighteen, Mosie's homeless, fatherless, blocked from his birth family, and a stranger in this forbidden world.*

Laura explained that he was naïve to our complicated English society of academic pursuit, electronics, social security, taxes, rent, cars, bills, insurance, and "wolves in sheep's clothing." There were some who'd already taken advantage of his gullibility. One insurance representative sold Mosie an expensive life insurance package. Another phoned him and weaseled out Mosie's social security number to sign him for supplemental medical insurance. He had no primary medical insurance.

Lynsey added that all the guys were from the Swartzentruber Order of Amish. "They're the strictest and most conservative order."

After cutting and cleaning up the tree branches and leaves, I invited the guys inside for lunch. Once indoors, they immediately were drawn like magnets to our family photo album. The pictures of our wedding, my husband and me in earlier years, the girls' as babies, school pictures, and family vacations fascinated lads who were prohibited the worldly "graven images." The entertainment that day was looking at our family history through snapshots. I realized then that they'd never hold their baby pictures or those of their siblings or parents. They had nothing except mental images.

Over the summer, my husband and I saw the guys a few times when visiting our daughters at their church. In October we were together at a Halloween party Lynsey had planned. Growing up without cameras, the guys indulged in what was once a sin — taking pictures and posturing before the lens all night. Crooked mouth. Crossed eyes. Contorted bodies.

The next month, our lives changed forever. My husband and I sensed a divine impression to take Mosie under our wing—an adoption of the heart. We discussed nurturing Mosie with prayer, encouragement, invitations for dinner, and the occasional greeting card. An assignment from God to simply love and help a young parentless adolescent. *Sure, we could do that.* An act of faith. We never realized all God intended for us.

On an early November Sunday morning, I heard the rumble of a diesel truck. Our windows vibrated to the sound. Uria pulled his truck into our driveway. Out he jumped along with Mosie. Both young men in jeans, western-style shirts, and boots. They'd agreed to visit our church then come home to Sunday dinner. Minutes after Uria and Mosie arrived, in popped Dan and Andy. I've since learned that where one former Amish goes, more follow. Being a social culture, it is common for Amish to simply show up at a friend or relative's home, walk in without knocking, and stay for a meal. When they leave the Amish life, most individuals continue the practice.

I leaned over to Mosie. "I hear that your parents don't welcome you because you left," I whispered. "Would you like us to be your English parents?"

With a nod and boyish grin he quietly stammered, "I'd l-like that." His thick, curly brown hair showed no signs of the Swartzentruber Amish bowl cut. I noticed his slender yet muscular physique. Husky hands. Large brown calf eyes hid his world of memories, pain, and passion. Anger.

Following our church service, Mosie and the others trailed behind our car, where at home I'd prepared a large meal for the hearty eating farm raised boys. Thinking they'd like homemade foods, I worked the previous day making a five-pound meatloaf, applesauce, cottage cheese, a variety of vegetables, and two loaves of bread. We gathered around our kitchen table and the four guys eagerly consumed it all. Then, as they sipped coffee from a second brew, they waited for dessert.

"We're going to be Mosie's English parents," I announced to the gathering. The ex-Amish and our daughters clapped and congratulated Mosie but, taking on a former Amish teen unsettled me. *Would he think it was too serious or permanent,* I wondered. My husband, Mosie, and I were walking blind into this veiled adventure.

Inwardly I felt apprehensive; *what am I getting our family into? How involved will we be with Mosie?* Besides, I raised girls. Didn't know a thing about boys. We're nonsmokers. *Did he smoke?* I'd seen enough Amish smoking at auctions to know it was a common behavior. Some smoked cigarettes and others took to pipes or chewed tobacco. Although Amish parents do not *encourage* smoking—children as young as seven-years-old sneak away to smoke—they neither *forbid* the habit. According to the Swartzentruber Ordnung (see Appendix D), which good Amish must obey, men are allowed to smoke cigars and pipes but their pipe must be simple, plain. No carvings. Cigars must be regular size such as Swisher Sweets®, and chewing tobacco must be Mail Pouch®, Beechnut® or Redman® brands.

Despite these apprehensions, we offered Mosie an informal adoption paper symbolic of our commitment to each other. "I'd like t-to sign it on my b-birthday, November twenty four," he said to my surprise. On that crisp autumn day, Mosie came to our home and into our hearts. The three of us signed the paper and we welcomed Mosie as a family member.

Thanksgiving Day and my December birthday brought newfangled fun with my family, relatives, and photos with a "son." Since he'd never experienced our parties, funerals, the ballet, Christmas lights, or an indoor conservatory, I often felt like I was entertaining a teen from another country. Those first months, Mosie remained quiet and stoic, a little unsure of himself, and yet I knew there was an ornery, rough young farm boy ticking toward detonation.

He was living in a dilapidated trailer with three other X-Men. Each time together, though, Mosie shared more about his life and began to reveal his explosive personality. His father used a "v-strap" as Mosie called it to beat him. The circular rubber strap used in the gas powered engine – known for its strength and durability – was his father's choice object when Mosie displeased him. Or when he needed to whip Mosie into submission. According to one Swartzentruber Ordnung, which good Amish must obey, parents are to bring up their children with "harsh discipline." They dare not show verbal or physical affection. No bragging. No acknowledgment for a job well done. To do so, they believe, would result in a prideful child.

"I can't remember being hugged by my mom or dad," he revealed one day. Eyes sad.

The Amish focus on strenuous farm work or in the father's trade. All work must be done without a chain saw, electric or air operated tools, riding lawn mower, motor operated lawn mower or any motor driven boat. Swartzentrubers may own stationary motors to do their thrashing, grind feed, run the sawmill or shop tools, and a washing machine. The rest of the motors must start by pulling a rope or a crank. It is against the rules to own a factory belt sander. If a belt sander is owned, it must be homemade. They are forbidden from driving any type motor vehicle, or operate any tractor, or bulldozer. Life on the farm is far from simple.

Early one morning, I phoned Mosie. "I wanted to ask if there's anything I can pray about with you." I overheard a whistling. "What's that noise in the background?"

"It's the wind. I'm up on a roof," he answered.

My mom instinct kicked in and I warned, "Get off the phone before you fall, son!"

Over time we became acquainted with this loveable, good-natured, industrious teen. It was becoming easier to "mother" him. He told us about getting in trouble with his father because he'd found a bicycle and rode it home. He explained that Swartzentrubers are not allowed to "touch a bicycle" because it has rubber tires.

"Why, what's wrong with a bicycle?" I asked.

"It's the rubber tires. But more important, the *inflated* tires."

"That makes no sense to me." I scratched my head. Another awareness of Amish rules.

Mosie described his parents and eleven siblings. "I'm t-the m-middle of twelve kits." He told me that he'd wanted to leave since he was sixteen but waited until he was eighteen.

He shared that his first year out was his wild, party year. Shedding the rigid rules of his upbringing, he co-rented a small house with four former Amish, who lived to drink on weekends. Some of his housemates took to carousing and sexual promiscuity.

"I took lots of pictures," as he'd been denied a camera when Amish. He showed me some of the pictures. Many exhibited him and his new "wayward" friends with beer bottles, or flipping the middle finger. Blue jeans. Cowboy hats. Big belt buckles. And buzzed haircuts. Silly faced pictures. They imitated what they thought were behaviors of all young English.

New to our world, he'd struggled to adjust with less structure, where no one was telling him what to say or do all the time. No supervision. And he quickly learned that freedom has its responsibilities. Consequences.

Six months from leaving the Amish, Mosie tired of his unbridled life. During this time of discontent, a new friend shared with him that rules don't make him righteous—*faith* in Jesus does. He began reading an English-language Bible, once verboten. His upbringing demanded a German-language Bible, and prohibited Bible studies outside the church. Since Mosie barely understood the German Bible, he rarely tried to stumble through it. Now, for the first time, he could openly read a Bible in English and grasp some meanings. A new understanding.

Patiently, Mosie stuttered his way through my machine gun-like questions each time he visited our home. I wanted to understand his childhood. I wanted to know my "son."

The first time I heard his relaxed, hearty laugh, he was playing a board game with my two daughters. The trio bantered with each other as if they'd grown up together. Siblings.

A "mom" love for Mosie sprouted in my heart. I counted the days until he'd come to visit; couldn't wait to hug him, talk to him, hear his voice. And his Deutch accent. It was like he was our natural born child. Sometimes he struggled to get words out; his stutter more noticeable when he felt stressed. Our daughters dropped in more often to visit their "brother" and our extended family members, excited about the addition, called for Mosie updates. And like other parents, our hearts broke when, on Christmas Eve, we learned our son was laid off his construction job. No work. No insurance. Little savings. No experience completing a job application. No GED, which our society values.

Clueless but wanting to help I asked, "What do you like to do Mosie?"

"Work with horses. I g-grew up on a farm with f-fifteen; some were road horses and some field horses," he answered. "We had names for t-them. One was Marcy. She was the fast one. She was the one I hitched up when w-we were late for church."

"I don't know a horse farm around where you can work." My mind raced. How can I help him find winter work? I'm city-born and raised and don't know about horse farms.

Christmas to us is a family time. We knew Mosie's biological family rejected him for leaving, so we invited him to spend the day with us. Through the flutter of gifts and wrapping paper, we shared love with our new family member. It was his first Christmas in an English home. Quiet and observant, he sat on the floor watching us pass gifts and open cards. Looking a bit confused, he commented, "We don't give cards."

"Amish don't give Christmas cards? Do they decorate?"

"Nah."

Later in the day, as our family settled down to relax in front of the TV, Mosie grabbed a third piece of pie and bounded down the stairs to our family room. With one leap, he jumped over my coffee table and landed on the sofa next to me. "I'd like to g-get my GED." I knew the Amish complete their formal education at eighth grade. Then they work in the family business or are hired out to others.

"We'll see what it takes to get you enrolled." This would be a new learning curve for me. Everyone in my family had a minimum college-level education. I didn't know how or who to contact about a GED. *Did it cost? Where were classes?* Schooling was a natural part of my childhood, so my work was cut out for me with Mosie and, I was determined to support him if he wanted to continue his education. I planned to make calls to our Board of Education. Later, I discovered the local GED preparation program.

Christmas closed with great memories, and Mosie went back to his dilapidated trailer-home.

The week between Christmas and New Year's Day is always a downer to me. Uneventful. Boring. Not that year.

December 27, 2009—two nights after Christmas—my husband and I huddled together on the sofa during a winter snow storm. Our daughters were at their own parties. Mosie out doing his thing. The two of us were passing time watching TV when the phone rang.

"We don't know where Mosie is!" anxiously announced his trailer-mate, Dan. "I've called everywhere, no one has seen him."

After frantic calls to his friends whom I'd met, and to my daughters, we learned the frightening news all parents fear. Mosie slid on black ice and was taken by ambulance to an Emergency Department of a hospital. Although it was slick, dark, and roads were closed due to weather, my husband and I drove to the hospital to see our son. No weather warning was going to keep me away. I wanted to know for myself that he was okay.

We scrambled into the Emergency Department to find Mosie propped up in a bed. Dazed. Broken glass shards in his ears and hair, and staples held together a head gash.

"We tried to find out who to call but we couldn't understand his accent," an ED nurse told us.

His totaled car was wrapped around an electric pole. He suffered a head wound and concussion. Although his trailer-mate expected to take Mosie home, we took him to ours to recover. I knew, from personal experience, about painful concussions. My husband and I thought it wise for Mosie to recuperate in our home rather than the dismally cold, ramshackle trailer with sagging insulation where he slept on a timeworn, sunken sofa bed.

Over those recovery days into 2010, Mosie called around searching for another job and a car. My husband and I prayed. We held our breath in hopes. I was impressed at the phone calls and offers to help from our concerned friends . . . and his. At that point, I recognized the powerful bond among former Amish. Their brotherhood supports and encourages one another. Several called, and came to our home to visit Mosie. Check in on him. *Must be a throwback to his Amish days. They're a relational people,* I thought. Within a week, we learned of a horse-boarding farm needing help and we drove Mosie out for a job interview. Hired. Then another ex-Amish friend, moving to North Carolina, sold his car to Mosie at a low price. Knowing Mosie had no car or income yet, his friend set up a payment plan. *Ah, a new job and a car. Things were settled again. Thank you Lord,* I prayed.

Since our local career center offered GED preparation classes and his new job was close to our home, my husband and I decided it'd be easier— and fuel efficient—for Mosie to live with us. We thought and prayed about it. Then offered, "You can live here."

As soon as he recovered from his concussion, and had his head staples removed, he transferred his meager belongings from the trailer to our home. I can still see him standing at the top of our stairs by the front door holding an 80-pound steel safe. "Where should I put this?" he asked.

"Down," I replied wide-eyed.

He hoisted the weighty safe onto his shoulders and toted it downstairs to our spare bedroom. I learned more about these former Amish; they all hid their cash in a safe. And I was learning about a young man's strength, boundless energy, and bottomless appetite!

Early each morning, our "son" drove to his horse-farm job as he adjusted to new life in our Nixon household. Eventually, I broached a subject I'd been avoiding. "Mosie, did your parents take you to the dentist?" I had to ask because I was tired of looking at the big black cavity on his front tooth.

"My parents sent me to a dentist once. When I had to get my teeth p-pulled out."

"Why did you have to get teeth pulled?"

"They were r-rotten in the front."

"Ugh, how old were you?"

"'Bout fourteen."

"You didn't go to a dentist regularly?"

"Nah. Chust that time. My parents sent me to an Amish d-dentist."

"What's that mean?"

"He didn't go to school. He chust read books and taught himself."

"What happened when he pulled out your front teeth?"

"I went to another Amish d-dentist that made me a partial." Then he flicked it out with his tongue. And grinned. *Eww, such a boy.*

Swartzentruber Amish don't honor daily dental hygiene. His Amish parents didn't seek outside dental care and they allowed Mosie to smoke. *Hmm, smoking, plus no brushing, plus not seeing a dentist equaled decay. Glad he quit before moving in with us.* I've since learned that deliberate inattention to hygiene is their evidence of righteous living.

"Mosie, most English parents take their kids to the dentist once or twice a year. Plus we teach our kids to brush their teeth every day. God gives you only one set of permanent teeth. You want to take care of them." Then I asked if he'd be willing to see our dentist. He hesitated. I feared I'd offended him. But he agreed.

Weeks later, I drove him to our dentist and flipped through magazines in the waiting room while he was seen. About half an hour later, he strolled out and I looked up, "How many?"

"'Lavin," he said appearing a bit proud of the number of cavities yet overwhelmed with the unfamiliar situation and its treatment.

"You have eleven cavities?" I was astounded. My husband and I made financial arrangements with our dentist to bring Mosie's mouth up to speed over the next several months.

"Don't worry son, we'll help you get your teeth right."

Spring again arrived—one year since we'd first met—and the church where Mosie and our daughters attended offered Baptism Sunday. Since Mosie had accepted Jesus as his Savior, he wanted to show his commitment through baptism. Before the big day he pulled out his Amish clothes he'd worn the night he ran away. "I wanna wear t-these when I get b-baptized."

I looked at the wrinkled dark blue Amish clothes. "You want me to iron them?" I asked, feeling honored to be so close to his heritage. I lovingly eyed the garments his mother hand sewed, admiring each piece. I gently examined the seams sewn with a treadle, rubbed my hand over her hand stitched patches, and I wondered what *she* thought as she tacked together her son's blue vest then sewed on the hooks and eyes. *How did she remember all the rules?* No zippers. Two buttons only on shirt fronts. No lay-down collars. Vest must reach the pants and must use hooks and eyes. Outer jackets must cover a few inches of the pants, and close only with hooks and eyes, and no collar. Pants must have buttons across the front. Two small pleats in the back of the pants. The belt over the pants must be 1¼ inch wide—no more and no less. Socks must be dark – gray, blue or black. But the gray can only be worn during the week.

It's against the Ordnung for males to wear underwear, or any type of pajamas. Two-piece store bought long johns are acceptable if the male removes the elastic from the pants and replaces it with two buttons. The top part of the long johns must be altered with buttons placed in front, the same as his outside shirt.

She must miss him I thought. *Doubt the path he's on.* My heart went out to her, momentarily I shared a kindred spirit with another, albeit distant, mom.

I didn't realize then, but Amish baptism is part of membership – a solemn covenant to the Church – to forever live and die as Amish. Now I understand Mosie's zeal. Then, I was slightly amused at his frequent reminders to attend this Christian baptism at his and our daughters' church. We went, and watched as Mosie stood on the platform with his pastor. In his plain, blue Amish clothes Mosie painstakingly read his testimony aloud to the congregation.

I am Moses. I'm 19-years-old. I was born and raised Amish in upstate New York. When I was 18-years-old I left the Amish to have more fun and live my life however I wanted to. I always thought English have more fun and when I hung out with my English friends I always felt happier. In the Amish, I was at the age to get baptized and I didn't want to be baptized Amish so I left.

After a few months out here, I realized that there is more to life than chust running around and making bad decisions plus I missed my family. So I started going to church with friends so I wouldn't be home alone. David gave me an English Bible but I didn't want to read it because I was afraid the Bible would make me feel guilty for how I was living. I didn't understand church at first but after a few weeks I asked my friends about God.

I started reading the Bible and discovered things I never knew when I was Amish. I learned that chust living by strict rules is not the way to heaven. A friend showed me Bible verses about getting saved like; we are not saved by works but by God's mercy. Then I prayed the sinner's prayer. God saved me. Today, I want to get baptized so everyone can see I am a true believer in God.

Then he donned his English clothes, he'd brought along, to symbolize the God of second chances and new beginnings. It was an exceptional day for the Amish teen turned English but, more importantly, he publicly acknowledged his faith-based life.

During later months Mosie told me more about the Amish "system," as he called it. His settlement preaches stringent compliance to the Ordnung (ordinance letter), which includes obedience to parents, and to tradition. "Being Amish and f-following the Ordnung and tradition," he explained, "gives us a hope of God's favor and heaven. If we had a choice between the Bible and tradition, Swartzentruber would throw out the Bible and keep tradition." He explained that most consider outsiders – English – hopelessly doomed because they're not Amish. Mosie's explanations answered my confusion about why Amish won't drive cars but hire English drivers—they believe they're avoiding hell by not driving the worldly convenience.

One sunny afternoon when Mosie came home from work, we sat on the back swing. "So what's your church like?" I asked. He looked over at me and smiled as he reminisced.

"It's called *Gma*," he answered. [Pronounced G-maay]. "We go every other Sunday to an Amish home b-but rotate h-homes. Sometimes it's in a barn."

Since church services are usually held in homes, the women vigorously clean the chosen home. Several women gather to wash windows, sweep, mop, wipe, and make everything sparkle.

I've been told that the mutual cleaning is a time of bonding but also that the hostess is nervous and fearful over criticism from the other women.

"The men and boys go in first, and most put their hats under the bench. Following them are the women and girls. They sit on hard w-wooden, backless benches," he explained. "All the men on one side, w-women on the other. We sing in German. The sermon's in German. Our Bibles are in German. Sometimes the preacher doesn't know what he's sayin' 'cause it's in German." Mosie smirked and continued, "He chust says what's printed. I always slept or looked around. The d-deacon w-was always watchin' us over the top of his glasses."

Mosie described the slow, rhythmic singing—sans instruments or sheet music—that lasts thirty-minutes. Musical instruments are verboten because "God gave us voices to praise him." In the calm, unhurried, monotone a single song can last fifteen minutes. I imagine the sound is akin to a monastery dirge or Gregorian chant. Many times, when our Mosie was happy or excited, he'd belt out a verse or two in German.

"After singing," Mosie continued, "there's a sermon—about an hour long. Preachers usually stand stiffly against the door." He said that foot-shuffling, nose-wiping, and in a detached voice, the preachers read or preach the memorized sermon. Most of the congregation, exhausted from a full week's labor and not understanding the sermon, falls asleep. "When the preacher went up, heads went down," he laughed. "An when the preacher sat down, heads went up."

Sermons, he explained, usually include the wrath of God. He punishes those who sin. A sermon might include stories of destruction befalling those who left the Amish. "Then scripture reading and a second-round of singing. Sometimes both of the preachers and the bishop would preach." At the conclusion, any business or engagement of a couple is announced by the bishop.

"Did you understand the German songs or sermon?" I asked.

"Nah." Mosie and I sat in silence hearing only the rhythmic squeak of the swing chain. "Hardly anyone understands the German."

"How long are your church services?"

"Three to f-four hours."

"What? That's long and must be boring for children. What if you have to go to the bathroom?" I stopped the swing with my feet. Not wanting to rush him, I awaited an answer. "Oh, we were allowed to g-go outside for f-fifteen minutes. Girls use the outhouse. Boys use a corner of the barn."

When children go outside, the watchful eye of the Swartzentruber deacon—the disciplinarian—is upon them. He makes a mental note of those who are away too long. Then after church or perhaps a week later, the disobedient ones are disciplined with stern warnings and expected to publicly confess.

Mosie inhaled deeply. Slowly continued, "I usually s-stayed out for half an hour." He started rocking the swing again.

"What were you doing for half an hour?" I asked.

He grinned revealing his white smile minus the cavity. "Smoking with the other boys."

I rolled my eyes and we climbed out of the swing. Went indoors. My lessons continued.

I learned that after the church service, the men file outside while the women remain indoors to set the tables with food. The men, following some chatter and smoking, rejoin the women. Eating is according to age, the older, married people eat first. After they're finished, the younger ones sit down. As the church is gender divided, so is the meal with men at one table and women at another. Sunday meals are always the same: bread soup, red beets, and pickles. Jams or jellies accompany the peanut butter. Everyone drinks the only beverage, water. The Amish justify the same-food rule as a prevention of competition or comparison among women.

The Holy Kiss – I learned – is another *Gma* behavior among some of the Swartzentruber and Old Orders. Just the awareness of the requirement was sufficient for me to never be an Amish wannabe.

Mosie explained that based on the "greet one another with a holy kiss" Bible verse (Romans 16:16), some Amish mandate the behavior. A Biblical scholar I am not, nor do I wish to debate the translation or context. I do believe what we read, in Apostle Paul's original letter, is a reference to the common custom in his day; a kiss on the forehead, lips, or hand as a greeting, affection, or sign of respect. It'd be similar to us today saying, "Internet hugs," or "Kisses to your family," rather than a literal embrace or kiss.

Within the Swartzentruber Order, typically the preachers and the bishop kiss in the morning church service or while they're in a separate preparation room prior to the service. However, some church ministers and bishops kiss anytime they meet each other, even in town.

Some churches practice a mouth-on-mouth kiss among members, while others do what is called a "cheek bump." Kissing on the mouth may also be practiced in some Old Order Amish churches. If a church requires the holy kiss, those who avoid it by turning the cheek are reprimanded as being "snobbish." Some discipline those who are members and don't make lip contact. Stories abound about the holy kiss on Sunday morning, from a girl who'd bump so hard that it'd cause another's mouth to bleed, to licking the lips before kissing.

Mosie added that in his settlement the practice is reserved for members. Membership is urged between eighteen and twenty-one years. Children and non-members aren't required to practice the morning's holy kiss.

Sunday evening is for the youth. Amish teens meet for Sunday night singing, partying, and sizing each other up as potential dating partners. The night singing is faster and more energetic than the slowly chanted songs from the morning service.

Twice a year, Swartzentruber Amish practice foot washing. It's a member-only occasion so the children stay home. Men and women wash one another's feet during a solemn ceremony representing humility and harmony among members. Usually the foot washing follows the biannual Ordinance Service where the Ordnung is read aloud. As with most rituals, there is some variation between churches, and between the different Amish orders.

While living with us, Mosie read his Bible in English. Then he'd often ask me to simplify words or a concept. I couldn't take anything for granted even his newness to Christianity. That became apparent on Easter morning when he stood in the kitchen and asked, "Mama, what does Easter mean?"

It seemed like one explanation led to countless conversations with Mosie. He taught me that the Amish suppress feelings and opinions with a "just deal with it" directive. But I wanted to encourage him to share his thoughts. "English usually talk about their likes and dislikes. I guess we value more openness." I realized he'd been repressed for so long that he either didn't recognize his feelings or wouldn't give himself permission to express them. "God gives us feelings. It's okay to have feelings. But we must be careful how we act them out," I frequently reminded Mosie. Then I'd ask, "What do you think?"

It was about five months into living with us before he ventured into unfamiliar territory of sharing his inmost feelings and tough opinions. I saw more of his emerging personality. I began to experience his moods that blew all over with the wind.

We were on the brink of summer that year. I stood in our kitchen and thought about the errands for my day and the recyclables to go to our town's Recycle Center. "Mosie, will you load up those recycle bins in your car and take them?"

"I'll put 'em in your c-car an take 'em."

Feeling uncomfortable with him—a repeat car accident perpetrator—using my vehicle, I repeated, "Put them in your car."

"You don't trust me. You t-treat me like a baby!" He yelled. His jaw set, eyes afire.

The "mother" in me wanted to spin on my heels and confront and correct his outburst. But, God checked my spirit. I realized that Mosie finally felt safe. As a former radio host and writer on parenting, I frequently reminded parents that kids will be honest and direct—albeit unpleasant at times—when they feel emotionally safe. Although it was a backhanded compliment, I believed my "Mose man" knew he was wanted, welcome, and free to respectfully share his opinion with me. "Thanks for telling me how you feel. I'm sorry if you think I treat you like a baby." He mumbled around a bit—probably stunned by my calm reaction. Shuffled his feet across my kitchen floor tile.

"You totaled two cars before we met! Then the one after Christmas. This is my only car, my way to work," I explained. "It's paid off and I don't want it wrecked. Or you hurt again."

I was realizing that Mosie, like the others, had grit to leave everything he knew. He had no preparation for life on the outside, lived with feelings of rejection, and needed love, kindness, and a bit of motherly guidance. He also had little understanding of the gravity of borrowing someone's car.

Since he'd received no hugs growing up, I wanted to teach him how to give and receive appropriate affection. I made it my goal to hug him frequently, even when he acted unlovable. I hoped to model our social skills. Most Amish speak to one another in direct terms without softening their words. By then, I'd met ones who were argumentative and, in a debate, stubbornly insisted they were right. Conflict negotiation and compromise are disregarded. By looking at his furrowed brow, I began to see when Mosie didn't understand the meaning of a word. I tried to explain words to develop his vocabulary and ability to communicate in our world.

The warm June days urged me out into our yard working on the landscaping. One sunny afternoon Mosie bounded in the door from work, kicked off his cowboy boots, and hurriedly hung up his hat. "Chust got paid," he yelled out to me with a broad grin. "An' I get to keep it all."

Coming in from the yard, I said, "You seem happy today." Washing my hands at the sink I asked, "What do you mean, 'keep it all'?"

"Amish kids must g-give all their money to the father 'til they turn twenty-one," a requirement he gladly left. His tone was matter-of-fact. I learned that in the Swartzentruber order, children become "of age" or considered adults at twenty-one. Giving all money to the father is an adhesive factor, fundamental in holding the young in the Amish life.

"Wow, maybe I should be an Amish mom so you can give me your paycheck," I teased. If our kids had to turn over all their income until they were twenty-one-years-old then I'd have a dozen of them, too, I inwardly mused.

We'd planned our family vacation to an Outer Banks island. When we'd invited Mosie to go with us to the ocean he replied, "I've never s-seen the ocean. Our family didn't take vacations."

That summer we packed our suitcases and loaded up for a week of fun in the sun. "My family is takin' me to the beach," Mosie repeatedly sang aloud to himself.

After the long car ride and a two-hour ferry trip to the island, we arrived to the smell of fresh salty air. Mosie climbed the sandy embankment to our part of the Atlantic Ocean and ran arms outstretched. He met the bursting waves with a jump and open-mouth laugh. Instantly, he learned that ocean water is salty. The remainder of our first day, Mosie repeatedly hacked up and spit out salt.

We lived for a week in a vacation rental home and spent our days lazing on the sand. The pound of the surf and squawk of the seagulls filled the air. Mosie contented himself with exploring the beach and watching the occasional gal strut by in her skimpy bikini. I raised my eyebrows and gave him the "mom" talk about dating a good girl. When we packed to return home, we all sported sunburns that were slowing peeling into tanned skin.

Living with Mosie—having him live in our home—was a vertical learning curve about teen boys, and the Swartzentruber Amish. My curiosity was given free reign and I often asked him about his upbringing. The dating questions were prompted, though, after he probed my husband, "How do ya ask a girl out?" My husband explained our general practices, things we did on our dates, and gave Mosie suggestions on where to take a girl.

"What do you do on Amish dates?" I innocently asked.

"Go to the girl's home," he answered. Then he gave the Cliffs Notes: the young man rides his buggy to the girl's house at night, hitches the horse, slips in the house, and into the girl's bedroom. The two spend the evening together in bed. They hug and kiss but are not permitted to go any further. Before dawn, while still dark, the guy leaves.

"Ya gotta be kidding!" I said wide-eyed and dumbfounded. "No guy is staying in my daughter's bedroom as a date."

"Oh the p-parents are usually in bed so they d-don't know who the guy is."

His account of Swartzentruber Amish dating seemed too bizarre for me so I waited until a couple of other former Amish guys came to our home. They were Ohio Amish and may have had a different tradition than Mosie's sect in New York. I revived the discussion.

"Yah, I'd had 'bout three dates," said Uria. "What Mosie says is true. An' if you see the girl the next day, like at Walmart, you're to act like ya don't know her. Don't talk to her."

"Uria, you're pulling my leg," I said with a smirk.

"It's true! Boys pressure ya to date a girl. You can do it every other weekend, parents don't talk 'bout it and you're not 'sposed to talk to the girl after."

It's unlike anything I've ever heard. Research told me that Swartzentrubers are embarrassed of the custom and keep it top-secret. I discovered the stealth and personal details.

When a teenage guy wants to date a gal, he asks her. Often, though, he's coerced, poked and prodded by his peers. If the gal consents, the date is arranged. Usually dating occurs on a Sunday night, every other weekend. The couple may date every other weekend only. During the opposite weekend, neither knows the other's activity. The house is quiet and dark with the exception of a propane lamp's soft glow. The suitor goes into the female's bedroom and shuts the door.

Together, they climb into bed and turn down the bed lamp. The gal may have on a long nightshirt and the guy has removed his coat or vest and shoes. The one who has dated before "takes the lead." There is no board or sheet between them. They are not bundled – a common misconception. Alone and in bed, they talk, hug, and kiss all night. They must do nothing more, and not less. The parents rely on church teachings to keep the couple from sexual activity. During the wee early morning hours, the guy gets up, dresses, and rides his buggy home. The practice is called Bed Courtship.

If the teens succumb to sexual activity, they are supposed to confess the sin. Publicly in church. And await their discipline – usually a *bann.*

Should they meet the next week on the street or elsewhere, they are not to mention the date. Everything happens under the concealment of night. Nothing of human sexuality is discussed. I have seen former Amish blush at the very mention of a date, holding hands, or a kiss.

Mosie related a time when he went on a date where the girl "took the lead." It was during the month when his upper teeth had been pulled, leaving a gaping front section toothless. "I don't know w-what was in it for her," he chuckled.

For Swartzentruber Order Amish, the point of bed courtship is to provide teenagers a means of finding a lifelong partner who will follow church rules. Parents know where their daughter is, and they believe that the church teachings will keep the duo from having sex. Our teenagers socialize with the opposite sex on a daily basis at school, college, the mall, online, sporting events, or at parties. But Amish complete school and daily interaction with potential dating partners at eighth grade, or around fourteen. After that, they have few opportunities to mingle daily with others. It may seem that the pickings are slim. Sunday night youth gatherings, therefore, become the night to find potential dating material.

Higher orders criticize the practice of bed courtship. It's an old tradition that conservative orders stubbornly cling to, fearing that any change weakens their church and threatens their eternal souls.

These days we tease our handsome, muscular, industrious guys about going on English dates and *not* doing Amish behavior.

I also learned that human sexuality is never discussed. "Do you talk about pregnancy?"

I'd read in some Amish fiction books where the word "pregnancy" was used and I doubted its use.

"Nah. We don't say the word. If we s-see a big belly on a woman, we jus' figure it out ourselves." He shrugged his shoulders and walked away.

Swartzentruber Amish never discuss sex or birthing with their children, even when a younger sibling is born at home. As a mother, I was puzzled that they'd promote bed courtship without affording their teens any sexual information. My curiosity wasn't meant to criticize or compliment the culture but to gain a new understanding so I researched and put out the question to others, "How much did your Amish parents tell you in the way of sex education?"

Answers ranged from "nothing" to "Mom sitting down with me and explaining what it's all about. If I had questions she would answer me." One former Amish woman said that her education consisted of her mother handing her a Mennonite book to read on her own before she was married. Some others concurred with receiving a "day before my wedding" pamphlet. Some of these women said they weren't allowed to talk about periods. "Got my first period before I knew anything was happening," said one. "After that all I was told was, *halt dich frei fun mansleit* [keep yourself free from men]." She felt that command meant nothing to an innocent young girl who had no information about her body.

"Sex education when I was a kid," said a former Amish, "was observing barnyard animals." Those who remembered their "education" said it was from peers, animals, books, and magazines scanned in secret. Amish feel they have experience by "getting to watch" if a cow is birthing but nothing more is mentioned.

From Mosie, I learned that cousins are permitted to marry. "Doesn't that cause inherited physical and mental disorders?"

"Yah, I guess," said Mosie nonchalantly. "My cousin is married to her second cousin."

The Amish staunch patriarchal society gives men supreme rule. Fathers control their children until death. Obedience and respect is demanded. With eighteen years of this imprint, it was difficult for Mosie to accept a woman's advice or opinion. We argued. We got mad at each other. "God must have a sense of humor to put Mosie in a household of strong women," I often told my friends.

Mosie exposed my husband and me to intimate Swartzentruber rules that made no sense to me. He said that in his settlement, the men and boys used the barn as a bathroom. The outhouse? For the females. This may explain why I've heard more progressive orders refer to Swartzentrubers as "dirty Amish."

He talked about the subtle trends among teen boys. Even their teens have fads, such as encouraging curls at the end of their long hair, or wearing a hat over wet hair to flatten curls. I learned that married couples, forbidden from using birth control, are publicly disciplined if they don't reproduce soon after marriage.

I began to understand why Mosie felt fearful and oppressed living as Amish. His curiosity, sensitivity, keen observation skills, imagination and drive for uniqueness were not valued within that culture. He wanted to feel special but being the middle child of twelve, he blended in and was often overlooked except when he misbehaved. Then his father whipped him. He'd never heard people talk so openly about their feelings and didn't know what to think of me and my family, who felt safe to express ourselves.

As the year progressed, Mosie worked, made new friends, and continued his GED studies. It wasn't always pleasant for us. My inner thoughts conflicted. *Did I try too hard? Was I too sensitive? Should I keep my mouth shut?* Often he seemed like a raft floating on a sea of uncertainty. Twice he seriously considered returning to the Amish. He'd become quiet. Moody. Or respond out of proportion to a situation. His eyes looked dark and his chin would stiffen. Despite the oppressive rules, Mosie pined for his birth family.

As the leaves began to turn and autumn made its mark in Ohio, I pulled out my seasonal recipes. One crisp fall afternoon Mosie strolled into the kitchen where I was standing at the stove. "What are ya d-doing?" he asked.

"Making caramel apples." Stirring the gooey, melted syrup I picked up an apple by its inserted stick and dipped it into the warm pot of caramel rolling to coat all sides. "You like caramel apples?"

"Never ate one." He stood agog watching me for this new English treat.

"I can't believe you've never had a caramel apple! They're an annual thing around here." I handed him the first of the cooled batch and he took a large, juicy chunk.

A grin crossed his face and, still chewing, said, "These are *gut*!" Within minutes he'd downed the entire apple licking his lips and wiping any remaining goo on his shirt sleeve.

In November we again celebrated his birthday – twenty years young. I baked him a cake, and gave the usual fanfare and presents that I'd give to my own kids. My daughters, son-in-law, and husband joined in to salute Mosie. To us it was no different; we always had a family celebration when one of us had a birthday.

"I've never had a b-birthday cake." He looked a bit restrained as he circled the table with his cake and gifts.

"Why?" I asked amazed at his statement.

"Birthdays were simply another workday." His eyes ogling the large sheet cake with icing and his name scribbled atop. "Can I blow out the candles now?"

By December of that year, we learned of a small available rental house across town.

"Mosie, you and your cousin could move into it and still be close to work and school." Equipped with a job, car, insurance, steady income, and more self-confidence, Mosie packed his bags and moved to the nearby house. My husband and I felt we'd done all we could to "parent" him in that first, turbulent year where he needed physical healing, and some material goods, a launch on his GED, a safe home and a feeling of belongingness. We kept in touch and he'd frequently stop in for a "mom" dinner and a hug.

Mosie texted one day, "I'm moving to North Carolina."

Later, he'd stop in with his loaded car ready for the trip.

"Where are you going to live and work?" I asked.

He told me about a construction job and his childhood friend, Joe, who also left the Amish. "Joe has a job for me and I can live in his trailer."

My heart weighed heavy thinking of the long move out of state and my "son's" future. We hugged – long. Mosie's eyes misted. "We'll miss you. Please keep in touch."

Weeks later, Mosie called. "I am living with Joe and working." A lilt in his voice revealed his exhilaration.

Months later, Mosie called. "I'm going to date Crystal."

"Oh, tell me what she's like," I begged.

Mosie excitedly described his girlfriend. His job. His church. His new life.

He still wanted to study for his GED—a challenge to those with English as their second language, and who weren't taught science, history, or advanced math.

In 2013, my husband and I drove down to NC to visit our Mosie. His stuttering had lessened. A pleasant surprise. His English and spelling improved as well as his outward respect for us. Our "son" was maturing.

During our stay, Mosie introduced us to his new friends and Crystal's parents. "These are my English parents," he boasted about us.

On the drive back home to Ohio, I smiled as I reminisced. "Wow, he's really a nice young man," I said to my husband. "Although his girlfriend and her family got the improved version—not the one we first met." I glanced over at my husband – smirking.

"Yea," he agreed. Further down the soft spring-green Kentucky roads, he added, "They should've met him a few years ago. But we get to see the outcome of our efforts. He's mellowing and moving on."

Bitter – sweet. I missed my first ex-Amish "son." Held onto memories of him living in our home. Was delighted and gratified that he was assimilating successfully in the "forbidden" English world.

Valentine's Day. Mosie called, "I asked Crystal to marry me." His voice was strong and confident. Happy. "Will you be the parents of the groom?"

"I'd be honored, son," I answered. My heart thumped hard with excitement.

We traveled down to NC and witnessed a beautiful, spiritual, sentimental outdoor ceremony. To cherish and remember each moment, I later penned the blog post "Ex-Amish Mosie's English Wedding" – along with pictures – where I described the day, the couple, and the tears of happiness. I wanted all my blog readers to share in our joyous memories, and good wishes for Mosie's future.

"However motherhood comes to you, it's a miracle." ~ Valerie Harper

Chapter 2

Harvey

Murder, corruption, sirens, and chaos were real in Jim's life. He'd served fifteen years as a Sargent in the New York City Police Department. When he retired, Jim and his wife Bea yearned for a slower, quieter life so they bought the farm—a twenty-acre one near Sullivan, Ohio. Their property sat across from a Swartzentruber Amish family.

A large, imposing man, I thought of Jim at our first meeting. With his booming voice, narrow eyes, and bushy eyebrows he must have been well-matched for his job in the NYPD. Shorter Bea, plump and pleasant, wore her silvery hair loose around her face. Both were energetic. Talkative. Honest. Funny. When my husband and I first met the couple, they were like a conversation tag-team. As soon as one spoke, the other jumped in with a comment.

Jim is Greek and his wife German. "If a Greek doesn't marry another Greek, they marry German," joked Jim when we met. He winked at Bea.

"We're the only ones stupid enough to get into two World Wars," added Bea. "The Greek makes the money and the German holds on to it." She glanced at Jim with a smirk. Eyes betrayed her tease.

I wanted to revisit them and hear about their decade-long relationship with the neighboring Amish family. "Let's get together at a restaurant," I invited. "My husband and I want to learn details."

The restaurant was crowded. Noisy. Before we were seated Jim began, "By the time we moved to Sullivan our adopted and two biological kids were grown and gone."

Bea added, "They moved on to their adult lives and families. So we were intrigued with the large Amish family living across the road on a sprawling 100-acre farm." She looped her arm through Jim's as the hostess walked us to our seats.

"Coming from New York City, we knew nothing of the Amish – only hearsay," Jim inhaled and continued, "We didn't know if they still shunned or what they did." He talked fast and piggy-backed one fact on another. "Within a few days we were outdoors investigating our new property. As we stood in the back yard looking over the tall weeds, a dour, stout, bearded man in black clothing and a straw hat shuffled up to us. He stroked his long, white beard. 'I'm Harvey,' the man said outstretching his large, calloused hand."

He remembered that they talked a while, learned Harvey was the settlement's bishop, and then watched as he wandered across the dusty road and down a long gravel path to his white, two-story farm house. "Days later," Jim explained, "I was outdoors when I spotted a wee Amish boy with large chocolate eyes and ear-length curly brown hair topped with a straw hat. "In his denim-blue, hand-sewed plain pants, and a shirt with matching vest, he looked like a miniature adult." Jim laughed out loud.

Bea nodded in agreement. Smiled. Jumped in, "I watched curiously as he convoyed over with his barefooted siblings to fish in our pond."

The server interrupted us. We ordered coffee. All noise and chatter in the restaurant seemed to still as we focused on Jim. Leaned in toward him.

He added that he stopped his work that minute, to watch and listen as the children around the pond chattered in a language he'd later learn was Deutch—the Amish dialect. They giggled and cast their lines. Jim's cop curiosity got the best of him and he asked the littlest boy, "What's your name?"

"Harvey." The boy's voice easy and gentle. Friendly.

"So I asked, 'How many brothers and sisters do you have?'"

"'Twelve' he said. So my next question was, 'Wow, any more at home?' I loved his slow, distinct words and accent. He told me, 'I'm th' baby.'"

Jim went on to say that he asked Harvey if his dad was the Bishop he'd met earlier. And the wee Harvey said, "Yup."

Excitement. Jim was overcome with this novel opportunity. He said he yelled toward his house for Bea to come out and meet the little Harvey!

Bea stepped out their kitchen door. Watched – wide-eyed – at the picturesque simplicity. The oddly dressed little man-boy.

That first year, their pond was a magnet to the Amish children, who'd slip across the country road to fish. Jim said he soon learned, "the Amish don't understand the catch and release principle. Sometimes they'd nearly empty out my pond!"

It wasn't a bother, though. He said that each occasion gave him and Bea opportunity to get to know this small, sensitive lad. "He wasn't afraid of us," Jim remarked, "which was a surprise because the other Amish children were cautious and stood behind their parents when we were all together. Little Harvey was outgoing, more loving than the others. When I looked in Harvey's eyes I could see he had more depth, more interpersonal skills than his family or peers—"

Bea bobbed her head and interrupted, "Jim noticed that every time he'd wave at Harvey, he'd raise his hand and respond. I didn't know if the others didn't want to be friendly to an outsider or what because they'd always look away . . . a few might smile."

"To our surprise their social skills were delayed and uncorrected by the parents," alleged Jim. He sounded indignant. He looked over at Bea for confirmation. She shook her head and smiled. Patted Jim's hand. Sipped her coffee. Embraced the mug.

Talking on top of each other, they both said that they were, however, impressed and astounded with the Amish work ethic.

"Every day from dawn, each member of that family worked. No air conditioning in the summer. Layered in home-sewn clothes in the winter," said Jim. He said that the family took serious the Bible verse about "the sweat of the brow." It wasn't just that they *wanted* to work hard but, they believed that work *had* to be tough or cruel to please God. He recalled the evening he peered out his front window and spotted little Harvey plowing with a seven-horse team.

Bea interjected, "Often the men would be in the fields well into the dark plowing with lanterns . . . sometimes until midnight." She blinked hard. Paused. Sat down her mug. Began again, "I was amazed at the chores assigned to even the youngest children. Hanging up laundry outdoors. Gardening. Hoeing. Cleaning the barn. Hauling hay. Beating rugs. Gathering eggs."

Through the years Jim and Bea met many Amish people at local shops, auctions, and in town. "In many Amish sects, the women work like dogs compared to the men," said Bea. "But in Harvey's family, chores were well defined and many times I saw the family and children laboring tirelessly."

Jim jumped in, "That's where little Harvey got his work ethic." He smiled big. Proud. Eyes widened. "His brothers and a brother-in-law are hard workers, too." He added that they spent long hours talking to, watching, and growing in their affection for little Harvey.

"But," Bea added, "We gradually sensed he was unhappy. He seemed to be . . . in pain. Often he'd stroll down his gravel drive, slip across our country road, and quietly enter into our home."

"Since we never saw any physical affection among family members, we began reaching out to hug him and tell him how special he was to us." Jim looked down. Shook his head. Quieted. Emptied a sugar packet into his coffee. Stirred.

Bea filled the silence, "He'd repeat to Harvey, 'You're a bright boy.' He needed affirmation. Any child does," she protested. "When my kids got something right, I said 'good for you' and Harvey needed that but, I never witnessed any physical or verbal love from the Amish parents to their children."

Jim asserted, "Sometimes Harvey's siblings would venture into our home but, only after invited. They were mesmerized with our TV and electricity." He stopped. Gulped from his mug. Squinted his eyes, "But the patriarch's wife . . . would not come into our house. She still hasn't and it's been ten years."

Jim and Bea agreed they were charmed by all the children, and wanted to take pictures although they didn't want to embarrass or invade their private world.

"They'd turn their back when we tried to snap a shot," said Jim. "Little Harvey would stand erect and allow it." He snickered.

Bea chuckled and added, "We fell in love with Harvey. He was huggable. The others were too, but none showed appreciation for our affection. We are Greek. We show affection."

At first when Jim or Bea hugged Harvey, they said that he did not pull away but – "was unresponsive."

"He didn't know what to do," Bea added. "You get no hugs or positive touch all your life and you don't know what to do." She shrugged her shoulders. Looked at me and my husband. Waited for our response.

"So what'd you do?" I queried.

"We determined to hug Harvey as a model to show love," Bea answered. She explained that they worried that he might be "crippled later in life because he couldn't show affection."

"That's when I began calling Harvey my 'little buddy,'" Jim slapped his hand on the table. To an observant former detective, he thought it was evident young Harvey was detached from his own kind. His spirit seemed wounded. "I'd always see a lot of Amish kids in a group shoving, laughing, and having fun but, not my little buddy. Perhaps it was because he was the youngest, and he was small. Perhaps he felt left out. I have a feeling he was more intelligent. Most of the Amish boys who go out into the English world soon realize they lack in education." Jim sighed. Looked at Bea.

She rushed in, "I often asked little Harvey mathematical problems and he was right there with the answer. Harvey was born smart."

"But he was lonesome," added Jim. "He liked being at home and didn't hang with his peers or siblings. I wondered if they bullied him."

I could see sadness in this couple's faces as they remembered a harmless, gentle boy lost in a family of twelve children.

Jim said he got to thinking one day, *surely, there must be tons more Harveys amongst the Amish. How do they keep all these kids identified?* So he asked the bishop. The Bishop Harvey told Jim that all children are given the first letter of the father's name as their middle initial.

"Ya, they don't have a middle name," I said.

"No. All eleven of Harvey's siblings have *H* as their middle initial. At a family reunion or in church, Harvey H. is known as Bishop Harvey's son. I figured there must be some method to their madness," chuckled Jim.

Bea changed the topic, "Since we're smack dab in the middle of Amish country, we've attended many Amish auctions through our years here. We're constantly amazed at the invisible line between the Amish and English. Never the twain shall meet," she insisted. "Even with a barn full of Amish and English bidders . . . never would they intermingle." She shook her head. Friendly and outspoken, Bea admitted to always struggling with this insular culture and its segregated behavior. "You have to live with them for years to *really* realize they don't want to mingle with English on a personal basis." Her eyes met mine.

"So why do you think they're like that?" asked my husband when they rested.

Jim and Bea have lived sandwiched by the Amish for more than ten years. "I've come to believe the Amish worship the dollar more than they do God," said Bea. She rubbed her fingers and thumb together signifying money. Leaned forward in her seat. "They'd frequently ask us to drive them somewhere. It put us on the spot. Although it's a courtesy to offer money to pay for someone's gas, they never did. They were hesitant to pay for anything. It's the culture." She rolled her eyes upward. "Besides I didn't want to be known as the community's 'Amish Hauler' or 'Yoder Toter.' So we began to set boundaries."

I was surprised by her candor. Frankness. *Maybe that's her culture.*

Jim smiled. Sipped his water. Looked over at Bea to continue, "We felt funny at first asking for money but, most people who are schlepped a hundred miles round trip would offer to pay the driver." She pointed a finger at me, "Not them."

"What about Harvey?" I asked to guide our conversation back to him. I asked about his behavior. The couple explained that Harvey grew up and continued his admiration for their pond and TV. They said that he'd slip in on sweltering, humid summer days to cool off in their air conditioning, although it was verboten. He'd remove his Amish straw hat and chill in front of the TV. In the winter, he'd snuggle up to their furnace fascinated with electric and other English things.

Bea leaned back against her seat, "Harvey's home had two wood-burning stoves."

"I remember," voiced Jim about the day he was out near the road checking his mailbox. "The elder Harvey," he said, "was also standing at the road's edge to pick up his mail." The two men exchanged some friendly words. Soon their conversation turned to raising kids. Jim said to the patriarch, "I want my kids to be healthy, happy, and independent. Especially sons, they need to go out and be the bread winner, independent from the father and mother—that is Biblical."

"I want my kids to obey," the bishop grunted.

"You can raise a lot of kids but not all of them will do what you want them to do," Jim replied. Then he pressed, "What would you do if your Harvey met a Mennonite girl and got married?"

"No." Bishop Harvey stood firm. Shook his head.

Jim told us that he argued to Harvey that he must let kids go.

"No. No. No," Old Harvey stubbornly repeated, and then walked back to his house.

It was at the mailbox Jim concluded, "Harvey wanted them under his thumb." He claimed, "Amish want their kids to end up like a clone. They teach that submission to the father is equal to that of God, stressing the

Ephesians 6:1-3 verses about kids obeying their parents. I guess they ignore the Ephesians 5:31 and Mark 10:7 references to letting a son leave his mother and father and cling to his wife."

He confessed that his detective nature got the best of him. Another day he probed the father of twelve, "Why would you keep having babies?"

"It's our way."

"Why don't you immunize your children?"

"It's our way."

Jim chuckled. Paused. Scratched his head. "From that day on, every time I asked old Harvey anything baffling about his culture, the habitual answer was, "'It's our way.'"

"Maybe they just don't have the answers," Bea added. With a wrinkled frown, "I think they don't know so they discourage questions."

"So what happened?" I asked.

They looked at each other. Talked on top of each other. Said that after several months, they noticed little Harvey had grown into an awkward adolescent. His long Amish hair was bushy and wild. His taller body was lean, yet muscular from constant haying, plowing with the horses, and working with his father in the barn. The younger Harvey's patched blue pants and two-button shirt were always familiar – and welcomed. They continued to hug him. Gave him compliments and tried to build up his self-esteem.

"He knew we loved him. There was just a profound feeling between us," Bea admitted. Eyebrows lifted. She grinned. I thought if she could, she would've strutted with pride.

"But one day we realized," shot Jim, "we hadn't seen our Harvey for weeks. He hadn't come to watch TV or fish in our pond. Hadn't plowed the family field or been around the barn. I was worried and asked Bea if she'd seen him. She thought and then said that she hadn't."

Her mother intuition sounded an alarm.

His detective nose twitched.

They searched their property. The pond. The fields. No sign of the teen Harvey. They worried he was sick. Kept indoors. Then, the retired detective went across to road to investigate.

Old Harvey grumbled, "He's away for a while."

More days passed. No sign of Jim's "little buddy." He again questioned the elder Harvey only to hear, "He went away for a while." The worried couple didn't know what was implied.

Did he visit relatives? Is he working at another farm? They wondered. They worried.

Months passed. No sign of their Harvey. No explanation. They missed him. "Then late one night," Jim related, "We heard a light tapping at our front door."

Jim opened the door to the face of a clean-shaven, thin young man with short brown hair. He wore blue jeans and a plaid button-up shirt. Cowboy boots. Over the visitor's shoulder's Jim spotted an unfamiliar car sat in their driveway.

"I had no idea who it was!" Jim recalled in his vigorous voice. "Then it hit me, it was my little buddy. But . . . he held himself back. 'Harvey!' I cried once I recognized him. My voice was so loud and excited that Bea ran to me at the door." *I could picture that.*

Bea laughed as she reminisced. "He told Harvey to come in. and asked why he was acting so shy. It was sort of uncomfortable. He acted so hesitant I thought something was wrong. And of course he looked so different."

My husband and I waited. He took a sip of coffee and listened for the rest of the story. Bea swallowed her coffee and glanced over at Jim. Their eyes met. They both talked – simultaneously. Bea stopped. Jim won.

"Harvey was reluctant because he didn't know how we'd act," Jim's voice forceful. "He looked fearful. Said that he didn't know if we'd accept him since he left Amish—"

"Harvey," Bea interrupted, "said that he slipped out to the barn one night to make his getaway. He waited. Watched his parents' house for the lanterns to extinguish. When he felt it was safe and nobody was looking, he ran across the field to the road. Ran along the dark road until one of his buddies – who'd earlier left the Amish – stopped in a car to pick him up."

"Oh that's sad," responded my husband.

"Yes," agreed Bea. "He told us that he didn't relax and feel safe until he was inside that car!"

My heart sank with their description. *Why so desperate to sneak away? At night.*

Jim jumped in, "I asked Harvey, 'What were you afraid of?' And Harvey answered, 'Chus' bein' stopped an made to stay.' He was hushed and nervous even with us. Tongue-tied. We were thrilled to see him. We weren't going to criticize or condemn him."

I turned to Bea, "Did he explain what he did after leaving?"

"Yes," she answered. "He said that he went a friend's house that night and cut his hair."

"Whoa," I said. "Now that's an outward act of separation from Amish."

In their fervor the duo talked over each other. I didn't know who to look at as they both relayed the story – "Harvey's manner grew more positive the longer he stayed and talked to us," they chorused. Adding, "He admitted to partying, drinking, and living wild."

Bea said, "Harvey eventually become overwhelmed with many choices in the English world. He pointed out his once-verboten car in our driveway, and showed us his *worldly* cell phone." She said that they he'd already been to Wyoming. Worked construction. Lived a few weeks in Colorado, too.

"That first visit was brief because he didn't want to raise his parents' suspicion or get caught," Jim won out over Bea. "He feared a confrontation with them but, promised to return."

Jim, eager to know more, said that he and Bea exploded with questions. They held onto Harvey, hugged him. But Harvey slipped away to his car and into the night. And they wondered, *why hadn't the bishop told them the truth? Is it that shameful for a child to leave the Amish?*

"Then," Bea said, "he came back another night." Weeks later, they heard a light tap on the door. They swung it open and welcomed in the adolescent. That time they talked about his future. *Where would he live? What would he do? Was he dating?*

Jim, excited, interjected with a new matter, "Since some of his relatives are married to each other, we showed him what we knew. As professional dog breeders, we understand genetics and the need to outcross to bring in new blood. We drew a genetics diagram on paper to show Harvey why we can't breed too closely." He smiled. Stopped. Looked up at our server and ordered more coffee. "We explained the danger of human in-breeding and the genetic mutations that occur. It all has to do with genetics; nothing to do with God's retribution. What is happening to the Amish, is they marry Amish within their own sect, church group, or community."

Bea tagged on, "Harvey got it. He added that his sister married a cousin and had kids who never walked; they died young."

She said that Harvey listened and then changed the subject. "I have news," he told them.

A friend he'd met on the outside showed him in the Bible that salvation is a free gift, not something to be earned by keeping rules. Harvey said that he accepted Jesus Christ as his savior and was reading a Bible in English. Before he'd stopped at Jim and Bea's, he'd stopped in to talk to his father. He wanted to know if his *daett* [dad] understood what he read in the German-language Bible. But, his *daett* didn't know much. They argued. Harvey eager to share his newfound faith. The bishop resolute in his belief. He ignored Harvey. Communication closed.

Already, the news had spread through the Amish settlement. "Gossip is like a wind-fueled wildfire," Bea told us. Everyone was whispering, 'Harvey H. left.' "You know, it's a stigma when a child leaves. Especially the Bishop's son!"

"I'd heard that," I replied. Sipped coffee and questioned, the bishop was embarrassed for himself? Mad at how it affected his image? I'd be going crazy if I woke up and my child was gone. Would I argue at first sight?

"The family is looked down on for the child's decision. I think the father's really ashamed," Bea assumed. "We're just thrilled that Harvey was safe. Healthy. Happy. He still loves his mom and dad, and his sisters. That'll never change. He's a good boy."

"Bea and I will defend my little buddy when any Amish whisper to us about him leaving." Jim inserted. "They love to gossip and criticize."

Jim relayed that two years afterward, "Harvey's parents got word to him that he could come to a family auction only if he wore Amish clothes." Eager to reconcile, Harvey went to Jim and Bea's home where he changed from English into his former Amish outfit. "He had grown. Matured. Bulked up." Jim laughed as he remembered, "His clothes no longer fit. His legs and muscular arms bulged out from torn clothes like The Incredible Hulk. When he crossed the road to see his mother and father, we chuckled at the sight. They made him wear one of his older brother's vests so he had on 'proper clothes.'"

If this were a book, I thought, it'd be a page-turner.

Jim said that the following year, Harvey surprised them when he unexpectedly stopped by their home. "This time, he brought along a young lady. Introduced us to her as his fiancée. An English gal, Lynsey." *To Amish, marrying an outsiders is sin.*

"She's Harvey's compliment, his completion. Whatever his parents believed, I knew this girl was God's pick for Harvey," declared Bea with a broad grin. The couple radiated with pride. Believed Harvey made an ideal choice.

The server placed our bill on the table. Jim and Bea said that they enjoyed talking about Harvey but, their evening had to end. They faced an hour drive home. I caught myself yawning. The four of us stood up. Hugged each other. I wanted to hold them close. Affirm them for accepting – guiding – Harvey. *Thank you God for this loving couple*, I prayed.

After we paid and stepped outdoors, each reminded us that they were willing to meet again. *They're proud of Harvey, and like to talk.*

***

Good thing Jim and Bea "approved" of Lynsey—our firstborn. We appreciated their help in filling in the blanks on our future son-in-law's life and culture.

When Harvey met Lynsey, an RN, he was a construction crew foreman, with a sizeable savings account. Owned his car. Self-disciplined. Motivated. Shared a house with another former Swartzentruber. And nineteen-years-young. *Pretty remarkable for a kid that age.*

He entertained aspirations in our English world. Earn his GED. Buy a home. He was handsome. Well-built. And his soft-spoken, slight accent, and even-temper endeared all of us to him.

His parents sent him a caution letter—against his dangerous decision. My husband and I desired to meet them. I wrote. No reply. Another foreboding letter to Harvey. I wanted to reach out one parent to another. Wrote again. No reply. Another letter to Harvey warning him against marrying an outsider—Englischer.

"But we're good Christian people," I whined to my friend Karen at church.

"Doesn't matter. You are the wicked world."

"We've been married thirty-five years. That should show them we're stable people."

"Doesn't matter. You're outsiders."

"But we love and accept their son."

"Doesn't matter. You're English."

Their letters to Harvey never expressed sadness. Only reproof for his faulty decision. As a mom, I could understand their deep concern, their grief, and sense of loss. If they had these feelings, it was never obvious. Only their vehement opposition to this marriage.

Nonetheless, our plans for – and merriment over – our daughter's wedding day continued.

As I'd learned from housing Mosie, Amish dating is secretive, guarded, and cryptic. In my curiosity, I asked Harvey, "What's the Amish wedding like?" *I love learning about different cultures.*

"Usually the couple goes before the bishop," he explained. "If he doesn't find anything wrong or they're not breaking any rules, then he gives the Church's approval for the marriage."

"But, that's not the way with all Amish, is it?"

"No, but it is in my settlement."

Harvey told me that most Swartzentruber Amish marry on a Tuesday or Thursday in the fall after harvest. Historically, this season was chosen because the crops were in and haying was over. The cooler season also made it easier and practical to preserve wedding food without refrigeration. In the two weeks leading up to the wedding, the bishop warns the bride and groom to refrain from sex for the first three nights. The origin of this practice supposedly came from the apocryphal Book of Tobit about Tobiah (or Tobias) and Sarah. They started their marriage with three nights of prayer rather than consummating their marriage. Within the Old and Swartzentruber orders, couples may receive this marriage exhortation. But when asked, most don't know the story or why they're told to refrain from sexual relations. Those who follow the letter of the law will wait. Since they practice bed courtship, many have already engaged in intimate behavior. At their wedding ceremony, everyone sings hymns in German. The same melodic, a Capella chant as in church. *I imagine it is relaxing.*

As our daughter's wedding neared I asked a former OOA woman about weddings. She assured me that the preparation for an Amish wedding as less complex than English. The engagement – announced in church by the bishop – is followed two weeks later by the marriage ceremony. Planning consists of gathering friends and orchestrating the food. "The Amish wedding ceremony," she explained, "is a three-hour rite, but the affair is all-day." She taught me the German word for wedding *Hochzeit*, which means "high times" and that's what the couple, the attendants, and guests expect.

"Is that the custom for all Amish?"

"No, but it's pretty much the way Old Order do it."

"I've heard parents aren't welcomed to participate as much as English parents."

"No, parents help, and they pay for the wedding costs," she explained. "In my settlement," she continued, "the couple exchanges their vows before the church with the preacher and a bishop presiding. The bride usually wears simple, plain clothing much like her weekday garb. The groom wears his black pants and vest, with a white shirt." She described how the guests sit on the same backless, hard wood benches as they do in church. Women seated on one side, men on the opposite. The bridal party consists of the couple and witnesses—chosen friends or siblings. For the reception they add more positions – servers.

After the ceremony the couple and guests walk – if near enough – to the couple's new home. Awaiting them is an enormous spread of the best Amish food. Great care is taken to offer a variety and quantity of food, as hundreds of family and friends have congregated from all over the country. The married couple receives several presents including household items and tools for outdoor use. During the reception, emphasis is on matchmaking—seating singles next to each other. Guests usually stay through the evening. Late at night they play a game. The same at all receptions. When everyone has left – some after midnight – the couple is alone . . . to clean up the mess. *That part didn't sound fun to me.*

She continued with explaining that newly married Amish couples do not go on a honeymoon as English do. Since birth control is verboten, the young couple usually begins a family within the first year. I'd learned – and observed that – large families are the norm. *I know many former Amish who've come from families of twelve to fourteen children. And one from nineteen siblings.*

Whoa, I thought. So much information. Details. A culture opposite of ours.

Through other discussions with former Swartzentruber and OOA, I learned that the Church attitude about sex. It's for procreation – not enjoyment. The Swartzentruber Ordnung (see Appendix D) forbids married couples sex on fasting holidays including, but not limited to, January 6—known as Old Christmas—Good Friday, and Thanksgiving. *That would be too up-in-my business*, I thought.

Six weeks out from our daughter's wedding, we mailed an invitation to Harvey's parents. No reply. Jim and Bea responded to the RSVP and called to tell us that they felt sad for Harvey. "He deserves support on his important day," Bea told me. So in lieu of Harvey's real parents, he asked Jim and Bea to represent him, parents of the groom.

My husband and I prepared our attitude. We felt that the marriage would be intercultural. The upbringing of Lynsey and Harvey was polar opposites. Lynsey a city girl, Harvey a farm boy. She spent. He saved. She had a college degree. He an eighth-grade education. She was taught God's love and grace. He, a vengeful God. Opposite values, principles, beliefs. Nevertheless, we determined to support their union.

On the anticipated wedding day, Jim brought cameras and snapped shots everywhere. Bea lit the unity candle with me, during the ceremony. They beamed as they supported their "son" for this special day.

I made the mistake of mentioning the Swartzentruber Amish three-night abstinence to my brother. As a pastor, he found this information fascinating. As a brother, he teased. He kept miming to Harvey at the wedding, "Three days!" Then he drove by their home afterward. Spotted them unpacking their car. Rolled down his window and bellowed, "Three days!"

The Amish don't have *my* brother to rib them.

Months into their new life together, I queried my son-in-law, "How do Amish choose their leaders?"

"By casting lots," he answered.

"Is there just a bishop who rules?"

"There are two—sometimes three—preachers, a deacon, and the bishop." He added that they're chosen when needed; when one moves out of the community or dies. On the designated Sunday morning, the bishop and/or ministers go into a room. Each male member of the Church goes to the room and whispers the name of his nominee to the bishop.

Any male who receives three or more whispered nominations must sit in a row facing the congregation. The morning is tense, still, as nominees dread being chosen. They're admonished to accept the role as leader "willingly and not stubbornly."

A piece of paper with a verse written on it is placed inside one hymnbook. Several books along with the *one* are mixed and randomly laid on a table. Then each stoic candidate goes forward to pick up one hymnbook. He slowly opens his book. If it's empty, a gesture in his face and posture reveals his great relief. For the remaining others, heads sink lower as they dread finding the paper. Too proud to show their emotion, their heads held high but, their ashen face reveals their angst. The moment is strained as each one opens his book. The one finding the paper is *the* chosen leader. Even if the one appears stoic, tears fill his reddened eyes. The heavy, lifetime responsibility and inability to refuse the job is a like a punch in the gut.

"So your leadership is considered lot ordained." I commented.

"Yes," said Harvey. He said that upon finding the piece of paper in his book, the chosen one usually begins to weep. When he starts, all the others follow suit. Often his devastated wife weeps with her head in her lap. Other women rush to console her with clichés including, "It is God's will and must be. You'll get through it," while breathing a sigh of relief that it wasn't their husbands. "It's like a funeral." The wailing. The tears. "Like a funeral," he repeated.

"Wow, I never knew that's how you get your leadership," I observed.

Public speaking terrorizes most people. Amish are no different. The responsibility of standing before his congregation and preaching from the German Bible—often memorizing the sermon—paralyzes him. Harvey said that one of his uncles would seem to utter a million "uhs" and in a staccato pace try to preach while beaded with perspiration.

Whether bishop, deacon, or a preacher, part of the job requires confronting and disciplining those who break a rule. Harvey said, "Amish would rather ignore than confront."

"I know that for a fact. I've had former Amish ignore me when they didn't want to do something or answer a question," I said.

The lot ordained man must not appear more spiritual than anyone, yet he's expected to be an example. Provide for his family. Work the farm. Keep the rules.

That is just too much control and pressure, I thought. *Especially if he didn't want the job.* "Then what?" I wanted Harvey to continue. It all seemed irrational to me.

"Afterward they all go home for farm or household chores." Later in the evening, the men go to the new leader's home to console him, trying to get his mind off the colossal responsibility, and to help him get through the initial agony. The evening ends as solemnly as it began.

The bishop, his preachers, and the deacon believe they are special and God appointed. In most cases their authority must never be challenged. I asked how the leaders treat their community. Harvey said that if the man "didn't mind it too much, he was a nice bishop." However, if he was mad about it, "he could be mean, abuse people, or make favorites."

"Do the ministers or the bishop have any education beyond the required eighth-grade?" I asked. My husband and I have advanced theological degrees. His grandfather was a Nazarene pastor. I have ministers in my family.

"No. Chust the Amish eighth grade education."

"It's astounding to me that one who isn't divinely called, prepared, and passionate about shepherding a flock is accepted as a spiritual leader," I said.

"But it's not about spiritual guidance, it about keeping the settlement rules."

Harvey explained, "They're expected t'read books and know more than the others but since everything is written in German, they usually don't understand and give up." He reminded me that higher orders have Bibles written in English. I realized the great diversity within the Amish culture.

I thought of Charlotte, who used to teach in an Amish school. I valued her intimate knowledge. She once wrote me, "I have never yet heard of one *wanting* to be chosen, let alone desiring the gift of a bishop as stated in 1 Timothy 3:1. I am sure there are some who desire it, but more often than not, they see it as 'being led to the slaughterhouse'—to put it in their own words."

The role of the deacon is to watch and insure no church member breaks a rule. Harvey named some of the broken rules that demanded discipline, "If your hair was too long, or too short. If you left church service and stayed outside over fifteen minutes. If you trimmed your beard too much. Those kinda things."

Many former Swartzentruber and OOA have told me horror stories about their deacon, who's like a public school vice-principle. The rule enforcer.

Months later Harvey, Lynsey, my husband and I were watching the TV show, *Amish Mafia*. Harvey rolled his eyes and said, "There's no Mafia in the Amish. Anything near that would be the deacon. It'd be him who would go with the bishop or side with him on disciplinary matters."

"People usually think the bishop runs the settlement," I said.

"No. It's the people under the bishop – the deacon, preachers, and others who influence him."

"So can you tell me about baptism?" I asked my ever-patient son-in-law.

"It's a serious thing," he said, explaining that the solemn covenant is a part of joining the Church. He taught me that youth between eighteen and twenty-one are pressed to be baptized—a pledge to forever live and die Amish. A member's vow to the Amish church is more sacred than vows of marriage. Harvey had not joined the Church so I didn't have to worry that the leaders would try to get him to renounce his marriage and go back Amish.

Through the four years of marriage, Harvey and Lynsey have bought a house. Remodeled and painted the house. When Lynsey needs repair work, Harvey is there with the fix. Both work and attend a church near their home. During the years, Harvey has tried to make the two-hour trek to his boyhood home. He initiates with a letter to his father. Waits for an answer. Sometimes he has had to phone Jim and Bea for a quicker reply. They cross the road to ask the bishop if his son can stop in. *I've noticed that his father will receive a visit but never initiates one.*

While Lynsey usually offers to go with him, Harvey's answer is, "I chust want to go alone."

"Why?" asked Lynsey the first time Harvey turned down her offer.

"Because. I don't want 'em to be mean to you."

"How would I know? I don't speak Deutch," she mused. Shrugged her shoulders and left the room.

On one brief – prearranged – stopover, the newly married couple entered the plain, well-built *dawdy haus* and sat in straight, hickory chairs. The bishop and wife talked to Lynsey – in English. She told me afterward that she sensed no hostility. "Probably more like forbearance," she said. "But what's there to talk about? The crops. The weather. I'm ready to go."

Since Lynsey is a nurse, however, Harvey's parents appear to respect her profession. On another visit, his *maam* hoisted up her long, blue dress, pushed down her knee-length socks and showed her diabetic wounds to Lynsey. She asked Lynsey's opinion. When we mentioned it to Bea later, she said it was because they didn't want to spend money on a doctor. "It's always this," she said, rubbing her fingers and thumb together.

The last visit, Harvey's *maam* called Lynsey upstairs to a small, basic, wood floored bedroom. There, she handed Lynsey a threadbare suitcase. Laying it on the bed, Lynsey lifted the lid to see a collection of clothing.

Simple, blue hand sewn coveralls. Blue work shirts. A brown dress. White kapps. Woolen socks. A tiny white, cotton dress. "What's this?" she asked.

"I'm giving you his childhood clothes."

We never figured out her reason. To keep a physical connection? To show her love? To rid Harvey's things from the home? To help him remember?

Harvey told us that whenever he visits his home, he'll run across the road to the arms of Jim and Bea. Jim once told Harvey, "Whenever you look at us with those big, brown cow eyes, we melt. All you have to do is call us for help and we'll do what we can. We made a pledge to be there for you—no matter what. It's *our* way!"

"We know a mother and father can love more than one child, so why is it so hard to understand that a child can love more than one mother and father?"
~Unknown

Chapter 3

Jonas (aka Josh)

"What was the best part of growing up Amish?" I asked the tall young man. I strained to understand some words through his thick accent.

"They all help each other such as barn raisin'," he replied. "Amish make a lot of their own things like food, clothes, furniture, an a whole bunch of babies. They work hard. Kits are taught t'work for a living, no sittin' around playin' video games while expecting someone else t'pay the bills. Amish seem t'value family."

I first met Josh at church, about the time we'd become Mosie's English parents, and before Lynsey dated Harvey. Josh stood alone leaning against a wall in the sanctuary. He was lean, with a shaved head, and a firm, angular face. Through his narrow hazel-colored eyes, he looked down at me. He wore blue jeans, a western-style shirt, and a cowboy hat. Josh looked older, more mature, than his twenty-three years.

"Think you've met my daughter Lynsey," I explained.

"Yup."

"You come to this church?"

"Nope."

"Just visiting?"

"Yup."

It didn't take long for me to learn Josh was a fella of few words. I wasn't put off because he actually spoke more than Andy, a bishop's son I'd met, who'd left the Amish about the same time. Andy would simply look at people and grin. He texted more than he talked.

The next Sunday when I spotted Josh, he was alone again. I approached him and asked, "Remember me?"

"Yup," he answered poker-faced. This time I noticed his ruddy complexion. And I thought, *must be an introvert.*

Josh was surviving in a one-room hunting cabin heated by a woodstove. I hoped that he'd enjoy being in a home with room to move around. Besides, I'd learned that the Amish culture emphasizes family and food. "Want to come home with us and eat Sunday dinner?" I invited.

"Yup."

My husband and I arranged to meet Josh after the service. Then he could follow us, in his diesel truck, to our home. I was inching up on my vertical learning curve about former Amish guys. Their love of loud engines.

He walked in our front door, removed his boots, and quietly scanned our home from the entryway. He stood motionless, cautious, until I tugged him down to our family room. There, I showed Josh a small puzzle we were gradually putting together. He sat down and worked the puzzle—alone and contented. My husband and I went up to the kitchen and focused on Sunday dinner preparations before calling Josh up to join us.

Over pot roast, fresh green beans, bread, and applesauce, we chatted with Josh about his childhood. He hunched over the table shoveling in the food but, paused to answer. We discovered we shared mutual ex-Amish friends. It was no surprise. With their large families – Lynsey inherited more than 100 nieces and nephews when she married Harvey – all the Amish know each other or are related. Josh said, "I'm Harvey's causin."

"What do you feel was a challenge to being Amish?" I asked.

He cleared his mouth and began, "The worst part of growin' up Amish was tryin' t'follow all the rules—which is nearly 'mpossible as there are so many. Multiple rules nobody understands but, we're taught not t'ask why, chust obey. For example, we had t'wear black boots that were six-inches from sole to top around the leg. If it was higher, we had t'cut it down." I'd heard the six-inch boot rule. At a party, Andy sneered about the time, as Amish, he'd bought a new pair of cowboy boots. His dad took a knife and sliced each boot leg down so it was six inches from top to sole.

Josh continued, "Our clothes had t'be dark. Shirts had t'have two buttons. We had t'cut our hair by the rules. Trim your beard afore you got married. But after marriage, it's not allowed. Men had their rules and women had theirs. Kits must obey their parents in every petty thing or get in trouble. Anything outside of their rules is sin."

I nodded in acknowledgement thinking I knew about the Amish through my experiences with Mosie and Harvey. Josh was about to teach me more. I passed him the platter of meat.

"My name's really Jonas," placing meat on his plate. He cut it and placed a large chunk in his mouth.

"Why do you go by Josh?" I asked puzzled, listening intently. His accent was thicker than some of the other former Amish.

"When I left, I decided I wanted a new name." He paused. "A new identity." He swallowed. Cleared his throat.

"You wanted to distance yourself from your old life?"

"Yup." He sat back and contentedly patted his stomach. Finished and full.

"There was a man in the Bible who did the same. His name was Saul but, when he repented and became a follower of Jesus Christ, his name was changed to Paul." I offered Josh dessert. He claimed he was stuffed. I knew he'd love the applesauce—an Amish staple.

Inviting Josh into my home gave him the hospitality he craved and an opportunity for me to hear more personal stories to understand the culture. My inquisitive nature and love of learning helped me to get accurate answers I'd not find elsewhere. I knew that not all Amish are the same—diversity is the word. There are different orders and diverse churches with altered rules within a single settlement, too. Josh patiently explained and gave examples. One of twelve children, he suffered callous teasing and ridicule from his older brothers. They'd repeatedly pin him down on the ground, roughhouse, and tickle him to the point of pain. They called him harsh, mocking names. I wondered, *why didn't his parents interfere and correct inappropriate sibling rivalry.*

Despite uncontrolled sibling enmity, scorn, and torment, Josh nurtured the good times gathering around the table eating succulent meals with family. In one-on-one conversations, Josh opened up and talked. "Where I'm from," he said with his Deutch accent, "we were not allowed t'ride in a car 'cept for medical emergencies. Everything had to be done the hard an slow way. Convenience is worldly. Goin' fifteen miles t'visit causins on a Sunday was a two-'our buggy ride. An if it was ten degrees," he paused, "I'd freeze my nose afore I got there. Clopping ten t'twenty miles an 'our in a horse-drawn buggy with no windshield, made t'wind bite my face." He grinned, revealing discolored, neglected teeth. "Sometimes we'd put hot water in a plastic chug an put it under t'covers to help stay warm."

Josh snorted when he told me that in the winter, they could wear long, store-bought underwear but, they were required to remove the convenient elastic from the leggings. In place of the elastic they had to sew on two buttons to keep the pants up.

"What was your home like?" I asked as I piled up the food smeared, dirty dishes.

"In our house we had two wood stoves. One for cooking an one for heat. Both were downstairs an we slept upstairs." He shifted in our kitchen chair and continued, "Our rooms had registers where some heat would get up but it'd still get really cold durin' t'night 'til I got t'covers warm with my body heat."

I imagined the frosty winters where bedrooms had single-pane windows, little heat, and bare wood floors. Children are probably motivated to quickly dress once out of bed.

Josh continued, "In t'summer it was hot an stifling with no air conditioning allowed. Many nights I'd try t'sleep with open windows t'stay cool."

"I grew up without air conditioning, too," I added. "During the hot Ohio summers, Mom would often open the windows and position a fan on me and my sister. We slept in the same bedroom."

In the plain Amish home, most of the handmade furniture is passed down from generation to generation. Windows might have a single fabric panel and the walls are void of pictures. Most everything must have useful purpose. Simplicity is valued. The large kitchen is the hub of activity, where the stove provides food, hot water for baths, and heat to warm a body after chores in sub-zero weather. China or glass dishes are neatly tucked in a cabinet after they're carefully washed. No paper plates are allowed. When a daughter leaves the Amish, she surrenders her rights to *Haush-dier*—any home furnishings. When a son leaves, he relinquishes his rights to any farm property or parental support.

The home is where the family speaks Deutch and absorbs the rules. *Maidals* (unmarried girls) learn how to clean, sew, quilt and cook. Boys are given the responsibilities for the animals, and they work in the barn and fields. The verboten radio, television, music, and electricity keep the Amish from the allurements of the outside world. The children are raised insulated and supported by the Amish society so they won't feel secure or successful outside of it.

"'Nother thing," Josh added, "Amish are too tied up in the Amish religion. You can do only what is tradition an allowed by t'Church. If one wants t'be a truck driver, doctor, firefighter, serve in the military, or play football, that's not allowed." He abruptly stopped and sat silently looking disappointed. "Not possible without leavin'.'"

We got up from the table, pushed our chairs under, and went back downstairs to the awaiting puzzle. Josh reclaimed his seat overlooking the pieces, found one, and fit it into the emerging picture. I realized he merely wanted to have some choices. He had dreams verboten in the Amish life. He didn't *want* to leave behind family.

"When Amish," he offered, "I built buggies, removed wheels to grease, clean, an perform other maintenance duties. If cared for properly, a good buggy will last an Amish family 'til their death." He told me the average cost of a typical black buggy is between $1,300 and $2,000. Added to the buggy is the price of a good road horse—$800 to $1,500. Reins, harness, and bridle can cost around $500. Some Amish can pay "up to $10,000 for a breeding horse with a specific bloodline." On the high end, a Swartzentruber Amish man can invest $14,000 in transport. "Then, there's upkeep for t'horse, feedin' an Ferrier service. Runs 'bout $150 to $175 monthly per horse." The typical Amish family of ten children may have up to five horses and three buggies.

That's a ton of money, I mused.

Horses are divided into two purposes—road and field horses. Some orders may use a draft mule but, Swartzentrubers believe a mixed-breed is not a natural creation of God. The road horse pulls the buggy and will live about fifteen years. Field horses—Belgium or Percheron—live about twenty years and are for the heavy farm work like plowing fields. Harvey's family used a Clydesdale.

His description gave me more compassion for Amish when there's a road accident and a destroyed horse or buggy. Collisions can severely impair their daily life. Like our cars, buggies can break down and then the Amish either must walk or ask to borrow a buggy while their rig is in the repair shop.

I'd learned that far from being a cute throwback to earlier centuries, Amish are required to use a buggy for all daily transportation. They're extremely resistant to change or advancement. The "simple life" appearance isn't simple at all. Swartzentruber and conservative Old Orders have meticulous rules to obey. They believe the rules insure their unity and tradition.

With Josh's help, I learned that some of the Swartzentruber buggy requirements include (see Appendix D):

No type of battery lights on their buggies, or to have drum brakes. Nor are they allowed to have a triangle on the back of their buggies that indicates slow moving vehicle. Two kerosene lanterns, with red reflectors, are allowed for nighttime use only. During the day, lanterns must be kept inside the buggy. The entire buggy must be black. The dashboard must be 17½ inches tall. The Ordnung requires a total of six feet of gray reflector tape on the back of the buggy: two feet along the top, one foot at the bottom, and two 16-inch pieces on each side. The seat back must be 7½ inches in height. The buggy length and width must meet their stiff guidelines. Horse reins and harness must be black. Wheels must be wood with a steel band around the perimeter.

Swartzentrubers intensely forbid anything worldly on the buggy. No running lights, turn signals, windshields or mirrors. Historically, these rules emerged from the belief that protection comes from God alone. "These days," says Josh, "Amish keep all these rules because they believe this makes 'em righteous with God."

Our discussion of the methodical buggy rules reminded Josh of a lighthearted story. He told me that Anna would ride her buggy past the bishop's home every day. Sometimes she would hang her lanterns outside her buggy while it was still daylight. *What a militant!* I silently mocked.

We sat on our sofa and talked. A thorough question and answer session. Thank you God that Josh is so patient and not insulted with my curiosity.

I'd noticed that when a group is gathered for a barn raising or church, the surrounding field is a sea of black buggies. All Swartzentruber buggies are black and look identical. *How do they tell them apart?* Josh helped me understand when he explained that a buggy owner usually remembers where he parked. "Each horse is as different as our car is to us." Also, people peek inside for identifying blankets. Others go by the seat covers, as each is allowed to differ. Identifying marks such as minor maintenance variations, a rip in the back curtain, or a leak on the fabric from the kerosene lamp identifies one's buggy.

"So Josh, why did you leave?" My question seemed redundant but, I wanted to hear his perspective.

"Too many rules!" he looked downward as if the pain of remembering was too weighty. "Among the Amish, conformity—unity—is valued. Those who don't conform are made to feel unwanted." After a pensive moment, Josh added, "I think if there are easier ways t'do things, it's not sin t'try 'em."

Josh divulged that some of his confusion as an Amishman was "the rules are manmade—t'ministers an bishop decide—some loosely based on t'Bible an others t'save tradition." Swartzentrubers are prohibited from wearing sunglasses. However, I've been told by one that in his settlement, if he was driving a buggy facing the sun, then he could wear sunglasses. No clothes hangers. No music. No electric milking machines on cows. If an Amishman rolls up his sleeves in the summer, he must not show his elbow. Everyone is expected to obey the rules without question. Those who ask questions, disagree, or think for themselves are made to feel wrong or are ostracized. They live under a cloud of condemnation. People scrutinize each other to insure rules are obeyed. If not, they go tell the church leadership. *Big brother to the max.*

Since there's diversity among each settlement, both Amish and outsiders are often confused. Rules about pulling down the front flaps and side flaps are a daily mandate in Amish life. In one community it's against the rules to use the stormfront (windshield) unless it is cold enough to wear the thick cloak they call the *ivver-ruck*.

One example of the variable rules came from a man who "visited a neighboring community where they didn't have our rule." While there, he rode along in a buggy with the stormfront in use and no ivver-ruck. After he came home, he wanted to confess his "sin" in front of the church. The ministers told him that this wasn't something they would consider wrong, as he was just riding along with a person who didn't have that rule.

In the tourist areas such as Holmes County, OH or Lancaster, PA, most Amish interact daily with outsiders and depend on tourist income. In these areas – usually higher orders – visitors may see Amish driving tractors or riding bicycles – verboten to the most conservative orders. Some higher orders stay warm inside their buggies with propane heaters or, in rainy weather, they remain dry with a clear, intact windshield. I've even seen colorful running lights on buggies.

Their youth, like ours, push the envelope. Hide a radio and alcohol. *They can really pimp their buggies.* I've seen Amish teens dress up their buggies as English youth do their cars. A higher order may use horns and a speedometer on the buggy. Until they join the church, teens are given some latitude to live wild. After baptism, they're expected to "settle down."

I smiled remembering some of the fancy buggies I'd seen in Berlin, OH. Headlights. Turn signals. Dangling fringe. Windshields with artistic trim. Undercarriage running lights.

To the Swartzentruber Amish, following all the rules is the way to earn Heaven. But in the words of one of the founders of Methodism, George Whitfield, "Works! Works! People say you can get to heaven by works! I'd just as easily climb to the moon on a rope of sand than get to heaven by works."

After an hour Josh stood up. "Gotta go," he announced. "Thanks for the food an havin' something t'do on a Sunday afternoon. It was nice being around people." Then he headed for the door. I watched as Josh sped away in his diesel truck. Exhaust shooting out the back.

Our Sunday with Josh stirred my thinking about his pressure to conform. No originality. No right to question. No creativity. No exploration. All the qualities our society values and encourages are rejected by the Swartzentruber Amish. Josh was expected to replicate the traditions of his father and forefathers.

I'd invited him back when he had time. A week later, he knocked on our door. "Come in," I instructed. We sat down for warmed up left-overs and jabbered. I continued where we'd left off the week before.

"So what did you want to try?" I asked him.

He answered, "At fourteen, I dreamed of drivin' a four-door Dodge with a flatbed. I know that's getting' down to it but I share 'cause three years after I left, I was driving a four-door Dodge with a flatbed pulling a trailer!" He paused. Smiled. "I drove to Montana, Florida, North Carolina, New York an other states in b'tween an 'round Ohio." He looked out the window. Squared his shoulders. "Then I decided t'drive a dump truck. I got a new job to do that an love it."

"Gotta go," he stood up and announced.

"Already?"

"Yup. Things t'do."

We saw Josh often after that, either at church or with mutual friends. Gradually, he relaxed and became more talkative. In fact, I discovered that Josh was sensitive, tuned into his feelings, and willing to share them with me. Like the day he told about a contemptuous nickname his dad conferred on him. Since he's Harvey's cousin, I chided, "You're in our family whether you like it or not."

Since his parents haven't maintained a relationship with him, we included Josh at our family functions. After a large Thanksgiving dinner that first year, where everyone sat clutching their swollen stomach and moaning of being overstuffed, we watched a football game on television. "I don't know 'bout this game," he confessed.

"That's okay," I said, "I'm not too keen on it either." Then I took a chance, "Can you tell me about the night you left?"

He looked at me. His eyes penetrated mine. "I had a buddy who'd left earlier so I called him. I had t'secretly use the neighbor's phone." He looked away. Watched the TV. Smiled. I wondered if he felt a personal victory. Then Josh continued, "He lined up a job an home for me on t'outside. I waited three weeks . . . 'til details worked out. We planned for him t'pick me up one Saturday night an go to his house. The first thing was to cut off my long hair, take a shower, an get in English clothes. I had a hundred an forty dollars . . . 'nuff to get started."

"What about your parents? Did you leave them a note or something?" I thought again of my panic if I woke up to my child's empty bed.

"Yup. Put a note under my pillow." He got up. Went to the kitchen. Poured another other cup of coffee then returned.

"After you left, what did you do to live?" I glanced at the TV hearing Harvey and the others scream over a touchdown.

"My friends let me live with 'em for free. Gave me food 'til I started my job. They drove me around 'til I got my drivers' license. I was blessed with good friends." He silenced briefly while watching a football play. "It took time but, I worked my way up an six years later, I'm still learning." The game ended. Josh stood up, announced, "Gotta go" and vanished to his truck.

Five Christmases have come and gone. Josh joined us for each. Although he'd never given or received presents, he quickly learned our gift exchange tradition. When we rented a suite at a water park, swam, played games, and ate my homemade cinnamon rolls, Josh was there.

Summer bonfires included Josh. I've noticed a love of auctions runs through the Amish blood. The combination of entertainment, fellowship, watching who bids and how much, and getting a good bargain, fuels the enthusiasm. Josh, no different. He often revealed to us his "good an cheap" purchases. One summer night, as the family sat around the fire, Josh brought over his newest bid win.

"I gotta new gun," he announced.

"A real one?" our daughter, Laura, asked.

"Naw. It's a BB gun."

"What are you going to do with it?"

"For now, see how good it works."

We watched as he admired his new purchase. Rubbed the barrel. He pointed at the fire. Pretended to shoot.

"Now I'm gonna load in some BBs."

With his fully readied weapon, Josh pointed at a can near the fire. Pulled the trigger. The BB rolled out the barrel and dropped to the ground. Rather than a pop, we heard a poof, plop.

Then the barrel fell off.

We all laughed so hard tears were rolling down our faces.

"Great buy," snickered Laura.

Josh took it in stride. "Gotta find another auction."

Through the six years with Josh, we've noticed he – like other former Amish – frequently changed his job, car, and living arrangement. New freedoms. New choices. He's experimented with clothing choices and hair styles. Once he sported a mullet. Then blond hair. Brown. Buzzed. Long again. I've learned that given the once-elusive autonomy to make choices, many formers revel in decision-making. But not having childhood decision-making experiences, their skills are undeveloped. Some I know have made dangerous drug, alcohol, and reckless driving choices and live regretfully with lifelong consequences.

Josh stopped by our house one sunny afternoon. For the first time, maybe it was the sun, I noted a gaping scar on his head. "How'd you get that?" pointing to the wound.

"Got hit with a branch that cut my head."

"Looks like you should've had stitches." Nurse Lynsey would've seen to that.

"Maybe," he shrugged. "My parents never took me to a doctor."

Often when I've studied Josh – narrow, piercing eyes and solemn exterior – I'm reminded of the stoic Amish. Keeping a finger in the hole of their emotion dam. But in our home, I've invited Josh to freely express himself. Respectfully, of course.

His wry wit always tickles me. I'm stumped at how he seems to juggle his brothers' intimidation memories and family rejection with a positive outlook.

We've known Josh for five years and although he vacillates from financial generosity to "tighter than bark on a tree," we love him. He gave me a balloon one Mother's Day. Never acknowledged our English day again. He can be impulsive. He dithers around and changes his mind so often our family jokes with him to make a choice and stick with it. Once, we set a deadline for Josh to give us a decision. *He still carries inexperience in making choices. Once denied freewill.*

"I still wanna move up t'drive semi someday." He did—drove over-the-road for a year. Then, "I wanna be a speaker. Tell people 'bout being Amish. Maybe write a book." *It ain't that easy!*

"I also dream of being a cop or a caunslor [counselor] since God got me out of a bad addiction an habits. He set me free so I decided t'live for Him an do what he wants me t'do. I feel that maybe caunsling is my passion. To help people live a free, healthy, joyful life."

We support Josh, known to his Amish family as Jonas. His erratic decision-making? That's Josh and we love him. He'll gain confidence as he gains experience on the outside.

"Whatever you are, be a good one." ~ Abraham Lincoln

Chapter 4

Sarah

The telephone's ring jarred me awake. It was Thursday night, ten o'clock, and I was asleep in bed.

On the other end a young man's mellow voice spoke, "My cousins chust left. Can you give 'em a place to stay for chust one night?"

As I blinked myself into consciousness, I recognized the voice as Noah—a twenty-three-year-old who'd left his Swartzentruber Amish settlement years before. He lived in one of Ohio's many small towns thirty-minutes from us.

We'd first met Noah through a mutual contact, invited him to dinner to get acquainted, and soon after, included him in Harvey's November birthday party. That December, Noah called—he was in our neighborhood and wanted a place to stay overnight. We gave him a bed and breakfast. During our conversation, we shared about another town that was welcoming Santa. We thought it'd be fun and invited him to go with us. The childlike anticipation on Noah's face, as he'd watched Santa's arrival in the sleigh, was priceless. "I've never seen Santa," he beamed.

Now – a year later – his nineteen-year-old cousin, Sarah, left her Swartzentruber settlement and needed a place to stay. Her brother, Monroe, left also and was with her. Thinking of the drugs and sex trafficking in our county, I knew I couldn't refuse those so susceptible. My husband and I agreed to Noah's request. We heaved our groggy selves out of bed, dressed, and drove to Walmart to meet Sarah and her brother. She was tall. Willowy. Brown hair fell on her shoulders. Soft brown eyes. She wore blue jeans, a blue t-shirt, and boys' athletic shoes. I tried to imagine her in a plain dark frock, white kapp, and black bonnet. Couldn't get the image.

***

One inaccuracy I spot on fiction book covers is the lovely—or provocative looking—Amish gal with a wispy tuft of hair dangling from her white kapp. The two loose kapp strings flop on each shoulder. Her flawless skin reveals well-coiffed eyebrows. A slight grin displays straight, white teeth.

Those are fiction covers. If they were portraying the Swartzentruber gal, she'd be in a black kapp and bonnet in public.

Females are prohibited from the vain and worldly practice of plucking

their eyebrows or using make-up to cover acne. No wispy hair dangling—
every hair must be tidy and tight. Young gals quickly become adept at pulling
back and securing their hair by the letter of the law. The obedient female
keeps her two kapp strings tied under her chin.

Their culture teaches females must be subservient and passive, although
I've met out-spoken, opinionated ex-Amish gals. They have their own ideas
and often tell it like it is without using a mouth-filter. One gal proudly
announced, "I say it like it is." She does. Without a whim of who it hurts or
how it sounds. Mosie and Harvey have told me stories of Amish women who
run the family.

The kapp is symbolic of submissiveness. A black kapp is put on the
female newborn. All females are required to attend funerals in a white kapp.
Black is worn by young girls. Adolescent females may wear white. After
marriage, females always wear a white kapp.

Whenever she leaves the house, the dutiful female is required to wear
her black bonnet to cover her kapp, just as the man must wear a hat when
outside his home. Technically, the obedient Swartzentruber female wears her
bonnet to auctions, to garage sales, in town, and at barn-raisings. That's the
rule but, some females push the limits and resist wearing their bonnet in
public.

When my husband and I visited our son-in-law's Amish parents, I
witnessed the strict adherence to this head covering rule. Sitting in the
family's living room of their *daudy* [*dawdi*] *haus*, my husband asked if he could
see the barn. The father, a stout Amish bishop with a long white beard, rose
from his straight-back chair to accommodate my husband's request, pulled his
black hat from the peg on the wall, and placed it over his long hair. To go to
the barn on his own property, he wore his Amish hat.

While rules and tradition dictate that females wear their black bonnet,
they also use the bonnet to protect the handmade kapp, and as protection
from wind and winter's cold. Within stricter Swartzentruber communities, a
third head covering called the ivva-kapp or ivverbonnet is worn. Heavier and
warmer, the ivverbonnet is quilted material over layers of thick paper from
flour bags, and fits more snugly to the head. Some other ex-Amish tell me
they grew up in settlements where they never saw an ivverbonnet.

In some settlements the bonnet rules are more lenient. In the hot
summer, inside a black buggy, the bonnet may stay on the back shelf. I can
only imagine how hot it'd be wearing those things. Some settlements mandate
bonnet use year round while others hardly wear the bonnet in the summer—
except Sundays to attend *Gma*. In one Iowa settlement women wear colored
bonnets. And I saw – must've been a high order – women wearing flowered
bonnets. It's confusing to me. But I've learned this culture is diverse.

***

At Walmart, Sarah and her youngest brother – seventeen-year-old

Monroe – smiled in relief when they saw us walk through the front and approach the Customer Service desk. Each toted a plastic store bag with a few items stuffed inside.

"Thanks for picking us up," she said. I caught the absence of Sarah's bottom teeth.

"Where'd you get your English clothes?" I asked.

"We hid 'em in our attic while we planned to leave."

She and Monroe shuffled their feet. Eyes anxious to leave the store.

I perused Sarah and quickly perceived two of this young gal's immediate needs: clothes and food. "How much money do you have?" I asked realizing the many expenses ahead for her.

"I got a hundred dollars," she proudly announced.

I knew one of the reasons Swartzentrubers come out with little money is due to their rule that kids turn over all income to Dad until they turn twenty-one-years-old. Sarah's money was the amount she'd silently ferreted away from her dad's knowledge. I also knew that some children receive no budgeting or money management coaching from parents. *Hope she can stretch this out*, I fretted.

We loaded Sarah and Monroe into my car and headed for home. It was late and dark. My husband and I were exhausted from our day's events. I figured I could later find out about her other needs: her birth certificate, a Social Security number, a toothbrush and toothpaste, various toiletries, hairbrush, another pair of shoes. In the near future she'd need a bank account, transportation, dental care. Housing. A job. My head swirled as I thought of what I'd pledge for myself and husband.

"What do you want to do?" I asked Monroe.

"Get my hair cut."

Not surprising. I'd learned that the first thing Amish boys want – their first outward sign of revolt – is shedding the Amish long hair.

"Then I'll take you to stay overnight with my daughter, Lynsey, and her husband Harvey. He's ex-Swartzentruber, too. He has clippers for your hair."

We dropped off Monroe. Left him sitting inside on their sofa. I knew Harvey would welcome – understand – Monroe's wishes and needs.

Then we took Sarah to our home, gave her a brief tour so she'd feel comfortable in our environment, and tucked her onto a sofa for the night. I knew the overwhelming task before her . . . and me but, I'd deal with it the next day when I was energized.

I awoke thinking where-do-I-begin? It's overwhelming to teach and tutor a teen so much in a few weeks what our daughters gradually learned over years, I thought. Ex-Amish must feel brain-overloaded and wearied from learning. And those who are unwilling learners, stubborn, or argumentative have trouble successfully adjusting to the new "English" life.

As a Swartzentruber Amish, Sarah had consistently used an outhouse, wasn't allowed to shave any body hair, nor taught proper hand washing or cross-contamination with foods. I'd learned this order believes that ignoring their body appearance – vanity – proves their righteousness. Women aren't allowed to wear a bra. Menstrual pads? Verboten! During her period, many a Swartzentruber female uses rags. Wash. Reuse. Recycle.

The next day, my husband went to his job while Sarah and I picked up Monroe, now with short hair, and headed to our county's health department. "We need to see if either of you have a birth certificate on file. This will get you started in our society," I explained. *Good thing they were both born in this county*, I thought. *Otherwise, we'd be driving to another county or state.*

The clerk searched her vital statistics record and, fortunately, found one. For Sarah. "*Maam* always told me there was no birth certificate on me," Sarah exclaimed. Her voice surprised and delighted. She paid the fee and, for the first time in her nineteen years, held a copy of her own birth certificate. Many Amish parents deny their child's birth certificate in an effort to keep him/her in the settlement. And they'd never want it to appear they approve of their child leaving.

"Now it's time to search for Monroe," the clerk announced. Nothing on record.

"What are the steps to get his?"

She printed off a "denial" letter explaining it just meant he never had a birth certificate. "You'll have to take him to the Probate Judge to apply for one."

We followed her instructions for Monroe's birth certificate, then moved to the next item on our long list, which included clothing, shoes, toiletries, and a job. I knew how industrious Amish are and how Sarah would chomp at the bit for work and income. I emailed a plea to our church members, who generously and spontaneously donated items to her. Two of my pals, Karen and Vicky, contributed garage sale clothes. Lisa gave her a nice bicycle (but Sarah hadn't been allowed a bicycle so she didn't know how to ride). Some of my author colleagues sent checks to use towards Sarah's costs and needed dental work. *I'm so blessed with people who respond. No urging, begging, or manipulation. They just step up to the plate.*

This was my first experience assisting two ex-Amish at once and it was exhausting. I felt like I was tag-teaming. Her needs, his needs. Her questions, his questions.

After dinner, I drove Sarah to stay over with Lynsey and Harvey. *More her age*, I thought. *Sarah might feel comfortable staying with my daughter. Monroe could stay with us.*

Being an RN, Lynsey was diligent about teaching hygiene and, after giving Sarah a "tour" of their bathroom, she demonstrated the shower mechanics and the necessity to wash with soap.

"I'd like to shave under my arms," Sarah announced.

"Well, this is for you," Lynsey said as she handed Sarah a new razor. "Shave under your arms in the bathroom. It's better to do it with water or a shave cream so you don't get a razor burn."

An hour later a smiling Sarah emerged from the bathroom. "Here's your razor back."

"No thanks." Lynsey raised her hand against the instrument, "That's yours to keep." Our second day together – Saturday – I drove Sarah to a hair salon for her first-ever professional shampoo and haircut. She awaited her turn, conflicted with anxiety and anticipation. "I don't know. Should I cut my hair or not?"

"That's your decision." I flipped the pages of a magazine and patiently waited, knowing that Swartzentruber Amish rarely make choices independent from the group. I was giving her permission to make her own decision about a once verboten behavior.

"Okay, I'll do it." She heard her name called. Like a penned colt released for the first time, Sarah jumped up and bolted to the stylist.

Wow, what a change when Sarah dashed out of the salon sporting a short new do. With relief and newfound confidence that God didn't strike her dead for cutting her hair, she smiled, "I'm glad I did that." But after paying for her birth certificate and the haircut, her money was nearly gone.

Like many in her order, Sarah smoked cigarettes. "I'm trying to stop," she told me. But the stress of the new life aggravated her habit, which demanded more of her meager funds.

With Sunday coming, I invited the duo to our church. I'd already contacted several members to alert them to Sarah and Monroe's material needs, and knew they'd want to meet them. "Our church is different than Amish *Gma*," I prefaced, explaining, "Men and women can sit together. Our benches have cushions, the service is in English, there's only one sermon, and we sing with musical instruments."

To my relief, Sarah and Monroe chose to accompany us to church on Sunday, where several members awaited with open arms and warm welcomes. Lonnie and Joan each handed me bags of more clothing for the teens. A couple ladies asked Sarah, "How much do you charge for cleaning houses?" They made arrangements for transportation and discussed cleaning dates. *This'll make Sarah feel better and more independent,* I assumed.

Cautious about this new experience, Sarah and her brother clung to me amid the crowd. They answered when asked questions. Smiled frequently but quietly observed. We read our Bible in English. We clapped. We prayed in English. Men, women, and their children sat together. The children moved about within their pew. People said, "Praise the Lord," aloud. And we laughed. To them, it must've been a culture shock.

After church, my husband and I invited Lynsey, Harvey, and Josh to our home for lunch with Sarah and Monroe. It was a sunlit, warm April day. Anxious to get outdoors, we fired up the BBQ, spread out chairs and blankets. We pulled out the cameras and cell phones for new and fun photos. Monroe and Josh became immediate buddies. Teasing each other and comparing their muscles. *So willing to accept a new friend,* I observed. Sarah and Josh were attracted to each other. I enjoyed the atmosphere of anticipation of what was ahead for Sarah.

The next morning Noah called, "I found Sarah a place to live and a job in a restaurant." Again, I was reminded how the Amish are relational and their life of solidarity makes them quick to help one another.

Sarah jumped, clapped her hands and giggled at the prospect of a permanent living arrangement and income to keep. She snatched her plastic store bag and her few meager belongings from the two days with us and hopped in Noah's car. Together they drove off to her new home.

On Wednesday, three days later, I picked up Sarah and we drove to the nearest Social Security Administration (SSA) office to jump through government hoops in getting her a Social Security number. "Do you have a photo ID?" asked the bored-looking clerk behind the glass window.

"Nah," replied wide-eyed Sarah. She was beginning to experience the consequences of her choice to leave the Amish.

"I need proof you are who you are."

"Why isn't my birth certificate enough?" She said, proudly handing over the certificate from the Health Department clerk.

"It only proves your date of birth." She looked at me, "Go to the Department of Motor Vehicles and get Sarah an Ohio photo ID as identity proof."

Back in the car we drove miles to the Department of Motor Vehicles (DMV). Waited in a long line. Approached the counter, applied, and answered questions. The clerk snapped Sarah's picture. While we waited for it to develop, we pilfered through Sarah's few dollars to pay for her ID card. With that in hand, we headed back to the SSA office.

It had been a day of driving back and forth, waiting our turn, answering questions, standing in lines, explaining why at nineteen Sarah had no SS number, and signing paperwork. She eventually received approval and was issued a number. We were like two brain-dead zombies. Sarah craved a cigarette. My head hurt but we had to continue on our agenda.

We drove to our bank equipped with Sarah's photo ID and SS number. There, Sarah applied for her first checking account. Another round of waiting and answering questions. Then there were the fiscal explanations and strange words to her. More document signatures. It was nearing suppertime when we left the bank. I turned to Sarah and said, "Glad I have a flexible schedule so I can devote time to you. Otherwise, this whole day's accomplishments could've taken a week."

Sarah's first job and living arrangement soured. She stayed with a lady of the Melita tradition. She had rules. Strict rules. She scolded Sarah for cutting her hair. Told her she must wear a dress and a head covering. Not smoke. Must go to her church. Must clean her house and help cook in exchange for rent. The latter was reasonable, I thought. Sarah rebelled.

"What's Melita?" I asked Sarah. My face contorted with confusion.

"It's above Amish but not Mennonite."

The two females didn't connect. Sarah yearned for freedom, not more rules. At least not so soon after leaving Amish. The lady tried to make it work. Tried to be understanding, to be patient. She invited Sarah to family events and youth parties. Sarah wanted to move out.

Then, Sarah's boss reduced her hours in the restaurant's kitchen. Desperate for income and a more amenable – in Sarah's view – living arrangement, she hurriedly made friends with other same-age girls and moved to their house. She stayed with them for two months while looking for a more lasting living arrangement. I prayed for her.

Without a driver's license, Sarah was dependent on me or another former Amish friend – Anna – to tote her around town. Sarah's behavior didn't surprise me. I'd observed many formers who were transient at first. Who frequently moved or change jobs. I chalked it up as them exercising newfound freedom of choice.

Between cleaning homes for a few of our church families, and Monroe giving his money to her, Sarah was able to piece together a sustainable income. Not enough to rent a place.

"Why don't you help her get a job at a fast-food place or in a coffee shop?" a well-meaning friend asked.

"*Fast* food. That's counter-cultural to her," I explained. Swartzentruber Amish know nothing about working in the everyday chaos of fast-food chains, or mixing complicated drinks as a barista. They're from a slower-paced, basic, homemade-food culture.

"Could she apply for housekeeping at the hospital?" another hoped to help.

"No GED. The hospital won't consider her."

"I know of a job opening but it's an hour away," offered a third.

"No driver's license or car," I pointed out.

"What about telephone work, like a customer service rep?" asked a fourth.

"About what? Sales? Technology? Plus her Deutch accent might interfere."

Eventually a middle-aged couple at our church offered, "We've been thinking about giving Sarah a place to live. We have a large home, private entrance, and spare bedroom. Besides we've often given housing to college students and visiting missionaries." I was relieved with their thoughtfulness and sincerity. Both are active church members. She the organist. He a greeter. Their home more spacious than ours. With Sarah's brother living in our home, we didn't have the extra space for her, too.

After Sarah bounced from house to house and job to job, she moved into this couple's home, and found part-time work at an Amish bakery close to her new residence. She was able to walk to work.

A month later, Sarah texted, "I got my temporary driver's permit." With money she'd earned and Josh's shopping help, she bought an old car. We used her car for driving practice. Many good laughs. Scary moments – running through red lights and tail-gaiting. Driving a buggy, Sarah learned, was different than driving a vehicle. Although it took her four attempts, Sarah passed her driver's test and earned her license. We cheered for her. Applauded her efforts. Complimented her tenacity. I could see Sarah's sense of freedom exploded.

Sitting together in a restaurant one day, Sarah said, "Ouch! I can't eat." She pointed out her lower gums. Reddened and swollen.

"What happened?" I ignorantly asked.

"The Amish dentist pulled them out."

She couldn't chew anything crusty like toast. Without her molars, she couldn't eat lettuce in a salad or grind meat. I hurt for her.

She told me that while other Amish will go to an English dentist, her settlement had their own — self-taught on an eighth grade Amish education. Unlicensed. Unregulated. When I first learned of this highly guarded secret I could hardly believe it. I knew the Swartzentrubers were the most punitive and insular, and parents don't teach daily oral hygiene. *But settlement dentists?*

After our discussion, I asked Harvey, "Did you go to an Amish dentist?"

"Yah," He said. "I went to an Amish dentist to have a tooth pulled."

"Did he use Novocain?"

"No. Didn't use anything, just pulled it out."

"It must have hurt! Did you cry?" I cringed.

"I wasn't allowed to."

My mind went to the Bible verse in Ecclesiastes, "He that increaseth knowledge increaseth sorrow." I regretted having some knowledge.

Other former Amish confirmed that they'd used their own doctors and dentists.

"I really want to get my teeth," Sarah told me.

"Well, if you're comfortable going to ours, I'll make an appointment." A few weeks later, I drove Sarah to our dentist for her first experience with a licensed professional. She looked around, signed in, and answered questions from the hygienist.

"Have you ever been to a dentist?"

"Our Amish dentist. He pulled out my bottom teeth just before I left."

"Did he have Novocain?" asked our hygienist.

"Yes. He gave me Novocain."

Where'd he know to inject it? I overheard the hygienist mumble.

"Did your dentist have any letters after his name or did you call him "'doctor'?"

"We called him by his first name. He didn't have any letters after his name."

Where'd he obtain the drug reserved for professionals? I wondered.

"He works only on Amish, not English," added Sarah.

Well of course, I thought, *English would report him for practicing without a license. And he can't dispense drugs without a pharmaceutical license.*

"We don't fix a cavity. Our dentist just pulls out the tooth."

That explained why I'd met many former Amish – especially Swartzentruber and Old Order with partials or full dentures. Those with white, healthy, straight teeth are usually wearing dentures. The current—and most sanitary—way to kill germs is using a dental autoclave or a dry heat sterilizer. *If the Amish dentist is prohibited electricity, how does he sterilize his teeth-pulling tools?*

Sarah avoided other questions. Looked away and found a magazine. I thought she was trying to cover-up for her settlement's Amish dentist – this well-guarded secret.

"Who is the dentist?" I probed wanting to know if he was dedicated to only dental care.

"He has a furniture store but Tuesday and Friday he pulls teeth all day."

I left it there not learning his name or location.

Knowing she had little saved money, and no insurance, and meager income, my husband and I had agreed to pay for Sarah's dental visit and X-rays. This allowed for her next goal – saving money to buy her lower dentures. She struggled between going to an Amish woman who makes low-priced dentures in her home and going to a professional dentist to order dentures.

"Dentures are so expensive," Sarah bemoaned. "We do what is practical." For Sarah, she saw no purpose in paying several hundred dollars for teeth she could get for eighty.

She decided to save money by going to the Amish dental lab. I was honored when she invited me to accompany her. A cultural learning curve lay ahead. I later posted about it on my blog, "My Amish Dental Lab Visit." It became one of my highest read blog posts.

Months after the denture experience, and with her new, white smile, Sarah went out horse riding with Monroe and Josh. The galloping mare abruptly jerked to the left and Sarah lost her grip. She fell to the ground with a thud. Heard a pop in her ankle. The sharp pain was followed with swelling. Josh brought Sarah to Lynsey's home for "doctoring." She tried to persuade Sarah to seek medical attention for a possible break. Sarah wanted to wait it out.

Josh drove her back to where she was living. The couple contacted me, "Can you come over and help us convince Sarah to see a doctor for her ankle? At least get an X-ray?"

I entered their living room to see Sarah on their sofa with a propped up, swollen ankle, and unable to drive. The three of us adults shared our concern and urged her to see a doctor.

"I'll wait to see how I feel."

Two days later I got a call, "Can you take me to the doctor about my ankle? It's still swollen and hurts to walk."

"Sure. When's your appointment?"

"I don't have one."

"If you're going to a doctor, you gotta have an appointment," I explained.

"Well, I called and nobody answered."

"The office is probably closed for lunch."

I drove to her home again, and the hosting couple and I explained about doctors and X-rays.

"I don't want to pay a lot of money." Her face cringed. I couldn't tell if it signaled pain or confusion. "I've never been to a hospital."

"Any one of us here will drive you," I said. I didn't want to pressure her, only to make it easier for her to decide. I sat next to her on the sofa and waited.

"Oh . . . I'll just have my friend Anna drive me to the chiropractor."

I've learned not to argue. Especially on medical issues or treatment. Most of the Amish I know favor natural mixtures and methods, and to save a buck. Sarah, like others, took her own path.

The chiropractor determined Sarah's ankle was sprained and she needed to rest. For days, Sarah stayed off her feet. Josh visited and brought her cards, flowers, and food. But once she felt better, she resumed her house-cleaning and part-time bakery jobs. All along, she struggled to kick her smoking habit. But at one particularly filthy house, she soothed her stress by succumbing to cigarettes.

"Have you ever been to a public library?" I asked her one afternoon.

"No."

"You can apply for a library card and then check out anything for free."

We made plans to go after work. I picked up Sarah and we went to the public library. Awed by the books, music, and magazines – all free – Sarah applied for her first library card. While there she spotted a display of attractive Amish fiction books. She smiled. "I learned about Rumspringa by reading those books."

"You never talked about Rumspringa?" I asked.

"Nah," she laughed. "It's fun to read those books but it's all so made up." She picked up one of the titles, flipped through the pages, looked at the cover, and took it to the check-out desk.

I learned that some Amish read the fiction books but only for entertainment.

She worked in the bakery and cleaned houses her first year out of Amish. Then Sarah was wooed to resign her jobs and work for her older brother in his flooring shop. He'd decided to leave the Amish. As a business owner, all his Amish employees had to quit. It's against their Ordnung to work for an estranged member.

***

With fear and apprehension, Sarah has avoided her Amish parents for two years. She says, "They argue about my decision to leave. Mom cries. They tell me I'm going to hell."

I encourage her to keep in touch with them. Perhaps she'll reconnect someday. Whatever the culture, I believe a mom's heart is always with her kids. And in the recesses of their soul, kids want to please parents.

My husband and I are grateful that Sarah, who was to stay with us for "chust one night" has remained in our lives. She lived with the church couple, who continues their unconditional love, for her first year then moved to an apartment with Anna. Her vertical learning curve leveled after two years.

She toots around town in her car. Goes to a church of her choice. Experiments with clothes she selected. Tries different haircuts, colors, and cosmetics. She works fulltime for her "new" English brother.

And she's engaged . . . to Josh.

I've come to this conclusion: Just as we don't *really* know life inside the Amish, those who leave don't *really* know life in our world—until they experience it.

"I measure success in terms of the contributions an individual makes to her fellow human beings." ~ Margaret Mead

Chapter 5

Monroe

Seventeen-year-old Monroe waited inside Walmart with his sister Sarah. The two of them just left their Swartzentruber Amish farm to live "on the outside." Meandering through the lonely store aisles late at night, Monroe fingered the ball caps, T-shirts, and clothing he'd been prohibited from wearing. But he'd already donned some of the forbidden English clothes—those he'd ferreted away in the attic while awaiting his night exodus. His parents never suspected he'd leave.

My husband and I felt like we were involved in some clandestine affair rushing to a secret meeting place at night. We'd made arrangements to pick up the duo and give them a safe home for the night. "I've never helped one so young," I told my husband. Biting my lower lip, I questioned the decision to harbor a minor.

"You didn't remove him from his farm. He chose to leave," my husband reassured. "And we aren't restraining him from leaving our home either." He pulled into the empty parking lot, parked, and turned off the engine. The quiet was occasionally pricked by the chirp of crickets. We walked inside looking for two teens.

Tall, slender, solemn-looking Monroe looked down at us from under a ball cap. His long Amish hair tucked up inside and bangs fell over his forehead. His blue eyes were full of mischief. At the hem of his blue jeans, I spotted his Amish shoes. He shot me a quick smile and we introduced ourselves. *So young*, I thought. We ushered the pair to our car.

Sparse traffic made for a quick drive. I turned around to the back seat and asked Sarah and Monroe about their parents. "How many children are in your family?"

"Five."

"That's small for an Amish family." I looked at these two sweet, blameless faces sitting quietly behind me. *Were they scared? In shock? Feeling guilty? Wanting to turn back?*

We dropped off Monroe for the night at Lynsey and Harvey's home, since Monroe had said he wanted his hair cut. Sarah stayed overnight with us. My only free room was already occupied by a temporary guest so I made up our sofa. Tucked in Sarah.

Wonder how Monroe is doing? He'd looked like a deer in headlights when I left him on their sofa.

The next morning – Friday – Sarah and I picked up Monroe for our visit to the county health department for birth certificates. The clerk issued a copy to Sarah since she had one on file. But none for Monroe. Instead he was issued a "denial" letter and given instructions on the next step.

"You'll have to go to the Probate Judge with this letter and apply for a birth certificate."

The three of us scrambled into my car and hurried to the Probate Judge. Obtaining legal documents for a minor proved more challenging . . . and frustrating than I would predict.

Aside from needing clothes, toiletries, shoes, and underwear Monroe needed a job and place to live. *He needs a home and I have one . . . he can live with us.* My head buzzed with a swarm of thoughts. Without his birth certificate, he couldn't get a social security number, and without that he can't get hired. Without a job he can't become independent and pay rent, buy a car, clothes, or food. I felt like I had an oversize, lanky, helpless toddler to nurture.

We pulled up and parked in front of the imposing stone building with its tall columns. Climbing up the steps to the county court building, I hoped the process would go smoothly. Inside, we emptied our pockets and placed their contents in the security tray before walking through the metal detector. Once cleared, we grabbed our things and found the Probate Judge Office.

"Can I help you?" asked the office worker looking up from her paper pile. A large wood and marble counter separated us.

"We're here to apply for his first-ever birth certificate," I answered pointing to Monroe.

She snapped a quick look of bewilderment as she handed the tall seventeen-year-old a stack of papers. "Fill these out." She turned to continue her duties.

Monroe looked at me questioningly. "What?" His eyes blinked.

I pointed out the line to sign his name, explained the legal jargon, and waited patiently. Monroe methodically printed, then signed, his information on each line. I already sensed he was compliant and eager to please.

"And," the clerk swung around, "you have to sign this affidavit that you're his sister," handing Sarah another form.

During the silence of completing their forms, the clerk leaned in close and whispered to me, "Why's he just now getting a birth certificate?"

"He's just left the Amish and doesn't have one," I mouthed.

Monroe handed his completed paperwork across the counter to the clerk. Exhaled deeply, looking eager.

We collected our documents, left the office, and descended the building's steps. "Well, that's one hurdle we jumped," I announced. Feeling accomplished, I added, "Now, let's get you some clothes."

I headed to a social service agency that would give Sarah and Monroe a clothing voucher. Once inside, I told the director of the teens' needs. She scratched some words on a piece of paper, checked a box, and handed it to Monroe. She directed us to the clothing store of the facility.

Monroe and Sarah flipped through the hanging racks of unfamiliar clothes. "How does this look?" asked Monroe. His eyes pleaded for help.

"What size do you wear?" I naively asked. Didn't realize that detail is used by people who buy clothes at stores.

"I don't know," he answered. "All my clothes are homemade."

"You have on blue jeans from Walmart. Look inside the waistband."

Monroe flipped it over, "It says thirty but, they're a bit loose."

"You'll grow into them. Thirty and what? There should be another number. The first one is your waist size and the second is how long you need."

"Thirty four."

"Alright, then let's look for thirty by thirty four in other pants."

An hour later – after searching and examining clothes that had once been verboten – the duo hoisted shirts, pants, socks, shoes up to the counter with the clothing voucher.

"You getting hungry?" I asked.

Both nodded.

We packed the clothes and drove back to my house. I warmed up leftovers and we chatted as we ate. We laughed. Compared stories. I filled them in on Mosie and Josh.

Within days, Sarah was employed in a small Mennonite-run restaurant. She packed her clothes – many donated by our church friends – and moved on and away. She wasn't far but, without transportation we'd not see her for a week.

Monroe remained with us. Since we had a temporary boarder using our guest bedroom, Monroe had to stretch his long body out on our sofa every evening. During the day he was anxious, feet shuffled, bored. He wanted to work. "But, son," I explained, "You must have a social security number to be hired."

Our next hurdle was a trip to the Social Security Administration office. Tuesday – five days after leaving Amish – Monroe and I drove out to the government building. His face lit up at the prospect of becoming "legal English."

A half hour later, we parked in front of the building, went in, and scanned the room. Others waited. I snapped a paper slip from a machine, which had a printed number. Monroe and I sat and waited. Watched a rolling announcement on a nearby TV monitor. Watched other people come and go. Checked the time. Finally, we heard our number called and we walked to a window where an agent awaited. I was about to climb another learning curve.

"We're here to get him a Social Security number," I said indicating Monroe.

"You must have a photo ID," the agent replied. Her voice flat.

Detached.

"That he can't get without a social security number," I replied looking at Monroe who had the deer-in-headlights look.

"We can't complete the forms without a photo ID," she repeated. Then she looked around my shoulder for her next quarry.

I stood firm waiting for her to help us. "We can try to get Monroe a state ID if your office prints a denial letter stating there isn't a social security number on him. Then we can take that to the Bureau of Motor Vehicles to apply for the photo ID."

She asked us a litany of other qualifying questions. We dutifully answered to the best of our knowledge.

She paused, looked intently and asked, "And *why* is his birth certificate stamped as delayed?" Tapped her fingers on the table.

"Because he just applied to get it. His mother had a home birth and didn't complete the form for a certificate nor social security number."

Holding and staring at Monroe's birth certificate as if it were bogus, she stated, "I can't use *this* one."

"Why?" I asked confused. "It's certified. See the seal?" and pointed out the raised circle. I shifted on my tired feet wishing for a chair.

"I need the letter from the health department stating Monroe never had a birth certificate . . . until he applied."

"Well, the probate court that awarded him a birth certificate kept that letter." I watched Monroe with his stunned deer look. His mouth dropped.

"Why don't you have it?" she pressed.

"I *guess*," trying to suppress my sarcasm, "the judge kept the health department's letter when he issued Monroe a birth certificate."

"Well, I need that letter stating the health department had nothing on record. That will be one document on our approved documents list."

"Can I call the health department and have them fax over a duplicate?"

"We don't accept faxes." Other people squeezed by us on their way to a different help window. Some looked at us with pity. Others gave us a grin of relief that they weren't arguing with the system. I turned away to look up at Monroe rolling my eyes in contempt at the system.

"I'll call the health department and see if we can drive back to pick up a duplicate letter." It was noon, my gut growled. I wanted to sit down. We'd stumbled in the government's obstacle course for more than an hour. I moved away from the window and used my cell phone to call the health department.

"You have to get that letter from probate court." The voice on the other end informed me.

Phoned probate court. "Can you make a copy of Monroe's birth certificate letter from the health department?" I looked up to see our agent helping another person.

"Sure, I'll fax it right now."

"Thanks but, the social security administration won't accept your fax." Hunger gnawed. Feet ached.

"Then you must pick it up in person . . . we close today at four o'clock."

I looked at Monroe. He'd given up and sat down back in the waiting area. "If we want to get that health department letter – the one the probate court kept – then we'll have to drive back."

I tore another number from the machine. Joined Monroe in the waiting area. We sat. Waited for our turn *again*. Watched the TV monitor. Watched other people come and go. Finally our number was called. We returned to the designated window. "Can I speak to a supervisor?" Toe tapping. My patience was tissue thin. *Go to the top,* I thought.

A young lady arrived and escorted us to a different window. She had chairs. We sat down and listened as she explained the delayed birth certificate was invalid to their office. Then she told us how the photo ID could serve as one criteria to getting a social security number.

"He must have that letter and a picture ID to get a social?"

"Right."

"If you'd just let the probate court *fax* the letter, it'll expedite this application today," I pleaded. "Then I won't have to drive all the way back to pick it up in person."

She paused, reluctant. Then divulged the fax number. *Good to have a supervisor.* I phoned my new "best friends" at the probate court with the needed fax number. "Since you stay open later than the health department, can you fax that letter here now?" I implored. Then we waited.

Minutes later the office supervisor announced, "Got your fax." *Whew, now we can justify Monroe's delayed birth certificate.*

"Problem is," she said. "We still need a photo ID on Monroe to process his request." Monroe looked defeated. Stared at the floor. His chest heaved as he inhaled deeply. Exhaled.

"Well, he can't get a photo ID without a social," I tried to calmly explain . . . **again**. "Can you print a letterhead statement that he's never applied for nor received his number; we'll take it to the DMV along with his delayed birth certificate."

"He also needs proof of residency."

"He's living with me."

"What document do you have that proves his residency?"

She asked us another litany of qualifying questions.

Then I remembered, "Someone mailed him a check to help with clothing."

"A personal envelope isn't listed as qualifying criteria."

"We have an envelope from the judge's office when they sent some other paperwork."

"That will qualify."

With a faxed copy of the original "denial" letter from the Health

Department, and proof of residency, the supervisor printed out her "denial" letter stating Monroe had no social security number. She passed it through the window to Monroe. "We'll probably be closed when you come back with a photo ID."

We drove to the DMV where a famished and befuddled Monroe said to the lady behind the counter, "I need to get a State ID. Here's my birth certificate," and he handed it to her.

"Are you eighteen years old?"

"No." He looked pathetically at me as if to say, "Now what?"

"Then, we can't do it unless you have your parents' signature."

I jumped in, "He's living with me. Can I sign as guardian?"

"Are you his legal guardian?"

"No."

"Can't do it."

"His parents are Amish. They don't approve of him leaving so they won't cooperate in signing a form to help him get an ID." *I'm tiring of jumping these hoops. Be nice. Be patient.*

The DMV agent looked at me. Called over her supervisor. The two talked in hushed voices. Then she turned back to me and said, "Even as a minor, Monroe may apply for a driver's license learner's permit. It has a photo. That can be used as a legal ID."

"How's that going to help?" I asked.

"He could use it in lieu of the state ID. Go take the written test for a temporary license." She pointed to an office adjacent to her. Then added, "I'll be here when you return."

Monroe and I headed to the glass-enclosed office. "I want to take the test for a learner's permit," he told the lady behind the counter.

"Do you have a social security number?"

"No." Deer-in-headlights look again.

"The lady next door said he could get a learner's permit," I interjected. "He needs it as a photo ID so he can get a social security number." We left home four hours ago for what we thought would take one. I was pooped. Exasperated. Ravenous.

She picked up the phone and called the office we'd just left. "Did you say Monroe could get a learner's permit?" We watched her nod and hang up. "You can take the written test." She pointed Monroe to a computer monitor and explained how to use the testing program. "And you have to wait out in the hall," she said to me.

I waited . . . in the hall. Gobbled down a stale cookie from a vending machine. Called my husband to explain our complicated progress. Thanked God I didn't work fulltime. *Help me be calm*, I prayed. With no chairs in the hallway, I stood waiting for Monroe. Shifting my weight. *Please Lord, let him pass so we can get what we need and go home.*

Another thirty minutes. Monroe emerged into the hallway beaming with pride. "Got it!" he shouted waving his learners permit in the air.

I checked my cell phone for the time. It'd been five hours since we left home. We couldn't make it back to the SSA office – too far away – but we talked about returning the next day . . . early in the morning. We headed home, famished and fatigued. I felt brain dead. Grumpy. Monroe sat quiet. *How can illegals can get a social security number so quickly?* I silently complained.

On Wednesday morning I drove Monroe the thirty minutes back to the SSA office. At least we'd be ahead of the line. This time, he snapped a numbered paper slip from the machine. We sat and waited. Watched a rolling announcement on a nearby TV monitor. We heard our number called aloud and went to the same window from the day before. Monroe completed the forms, showing his temporary driver's permit as a photo ID, and he was assigned a number. But only a temporary paper copy.

The following week we received an envelope in the mail with his social security card. I felt like throwing a party. "Keep that in a safe place," I warned. *Hope no Amish leaves as a minor. The public doesn't realize when an Amish leaves, his parents won't support any effort to survive.* I loved Monroe. Hated the bureaucracy.

"Now would you like to go to a bank and open your own account? And hide that social security card somewhere."

"Sure." Then he skipped upstairs to his room, vacated by our temporary boarder.

"What are you doing?"

"Trying to find a good hiding place for my social security card."

"You'll probably need it at the bank."

We hopped in my car and drove to the bank. Monroe and I entered the lobby. He looked around, eyes searching. At seventeen, he'd not been inside a bank before.

"I don't know how to write a check," said Monroe.

"We'll teach you."

I learned, from living with Mosie and my son-in-law, that former Amish quickly absorb information. They're smart. We approached a man sitting behind a desk. *This should be easier.*

"I need to open a new checking account," Monroe told the bank officer.

"Do you have a social security number?"

"Yep." He dug in his wallet and proudly handed over his hard won card.

"Let's get some paperwork filled out." He penned words, checked boxes, and turned the papers in Monroe's direction. "Sign your name."

After Monroe completed the required forms. We left for home.

That warm spring evening my husband, Monroe, and I sat on our back deck. Monroe practiced writing out checks – one to my husband, then one to me.

"These are legal, you know." My husband advised Monroe. "I could go cash mine." He laughed and patted Monroe on the back.

"I like mine," I said. "Monroe made my check for five thousand dollars!" I went indoors and taped it on the refrigerator and returned to the deck. "Now I have money if I ever go broke."

We remained outdoors eating our dinner and talking. We were learning about the life Monroe had left. "Can you tell me more about your school?" I asked. In some of my conversations with other former Amish, I learned that the one-room Amish schoolhouse is a private institution and operated by a Board. Their belief system is against a large consolidated school structure, preferring a one-room school serving children within the local settlement.

"I walked to school or rode my horse," Monroe said. "Amish schools have thirty to thirty-five students. I was in school with my sister, brothers, and neighbors."

He told us about the concentration on basics like reading, writing, and math. "Older children learn German."

Amish favor unity and solidarity. Individual achievement is discouraged, so interest in higher education is suppressed. This is one way Amish preserve their community and traditions.

"If anyone acts differently, or wants to do something not allowed," said Monroe, "the pressure is put on him. At home we farm and I worked with my dad in his cabinet shop. Sarah didn't really like the cooking and gardening, so she worked with my brother in his flooring business."

I understood why many of those who leave the Amish struggle in our modern world, with our emphasis on education and earning higher degrees.

He told me some things I already knew – Amish children enter school speaking Deutch. They learn English from the teacher, siblings, and peers. Most of the teachers are eighth-grade graduates who want to teach. Rarely is a teacher in an Amish school educated beyond eighth grade, trained, or certified. "My mom was my teacher one year. Another year it was my teenage cousin."

My thoughts turned to Charlotte, a woman who was permitted to teach in the Amish school although she was non-Amish. Charlotte had explained to me that the Amish schools – where she taught – took two days off for Christmas and two for the New Year. She said that Christmas is considered a holiday (meaning they treat it as a Sunday. No work). New Year's Day is not a holiday so they work on that day. "They also celebrate January 6 as a holiday, calling it Olde Christmas. They get together with family for a meal on these holidays and have even more homemade candy and popcorn."

In our conversation Charlotte said, "The thing that surprises an outsider the most about an Amish program, is the way they [children] recite. They sound like monotone machine guns, spitting out those words without an ounce of emotion and without heed to the punctuation. Needless to say, after an hour of monotone recitations, you can understand why most of the men attending these programs are asleep by the end."

She added to my learning curve. "I've noticed if the children feel comfortable with their audience, I would say it is more like hog calling—each one trying to outdo the other in volume. While the teachers give lessons, or plan school programs, homework is not practical to their way of life." Teachers send home a periodic grade card, which parents must sign and return.

"We never had homework," Josh once told me when we were talking about school.

I remembered many of the stories I'd heard from other former Amish of corporal punishment inside the school. One said that he was forced to kneel on a broom handle until the teacher dismissed him. Another said that the teacher made him stand on his tip-toes and put his nose into a circle on the chalkboard. *That's a chiropractic nightmare.* Physical punishment is also the norm. Many of the former Amish related stories of whippings. Teasing. Unimpeded bullying. One time Harvey said that he was ganged up on and pushed into a thrasher.

These ugly—abusive—experiences leave emotional scars on children. Those who eventually leave may struggle to earn a GED because of early school memories. I realized the rudimentary education of the Amish when Mosie once asked, "What's a solar system?" Another time Harvey asked me, "What was the Civil War?"

The Amish are intelligent and eager to learn, I thought. I've noticed many are visual learners. They need only watch or examine an object to acquire a know-how to succeed. Andy repaired my garage door opener. Josh and Harvey do their own auto maintenance. Harvey installed the dishwasher in his and Lynsey's kitchen. Monroe fixed the broken motor on his car's electric window.

Over dinner on the deck Monroe continued to educate us about his school experiences. When he left, he took his final year's school record. "Oh, may I see it?" I asked. "Like how many people have seen an Amish report card?" I said turning to my husband.

Monroe jumped up from the table and ran to his bedroom for a bag of possessions. He returned with his eighth-grade report card. I saw the "scholar" subjects: spelling, reading, writing, arithmetic, singing, German reading, German spelling and oral spelling. His teacher also noted his days present, absent, and tardy. Also Monroe's deportment was graded—usually with the letter *B*.

I admired the prized little card. *What a treat to hold in my hand.* A few areas that his teacher checked for "improvement needed" included "obeying rules, and whispering too much." *Shameful.* At the bottom of his report card, the teacher penned, "Above pupil promoted to at home."

The aired cooled as the darkness settled down on us. We ended our discussion of the Amish school system, and went in to the warmth of the house. I felt proud of our past days' accomplishments. Monroe had all his proper English identification. He mastered the test for his learners permit to drive. We'd started giving him driving lessons . . . in my car. After he found a job and saved money, he bought a car. But until then, he rode a donated bicycle to work. Growing up Swartzentruber, bicycles were verboten so my husband taught Monroe how to ride his new bike.

When Monroe turned eighteen, we celebrated his birthday. It wasn't difficult having Monroe live with us, he was clean and neat, respected our home, and helped – insisted on – cutting the lawn. I filled his room with balloons and wanted to make a big deal out of this milestone birthday. "You're like a dad and mom to me," he said to my husband and me. My heart beat hard. I smiled. Then cried. My husband gave Monroe a long, fatherly embrace.

Days later, feeling mature, Monroe packed and bolted out of our home and into an apartment with Josh. I was happy he stayed close to our home so we could see him on occasion.

After he moved out, my house was quiet. Too quiet. The only reminders were large, dirty handprints . . . six feet up my walls. I thought back to his beginning adventure in our world. Walmart. The health department. The Probate Judge. The social security office. A first bank account. The five thousand dollar check remaining on my refrigerator. Learner's permit. Driving practice. Sitting on our deck in the wee morning hours sipping coffee before work or late into the night. His start in the English world was like a wooden rollercoaster. A rough, wild ride.

I wondered where he'd be in the years to come. Hoped he would remain in our lives. Amusing myself, I speculated, *maybe he'll earn his GED and work as an SSA agent.*

"Patience, persistence and perspiration make an unbeatable combination for success."
~ Napoleon Hill

Chapter 6

Verna

"I was 'lavin-years-old when I told Mom I was gonna leave the Amish someday," she confessed to me. "We were conservative Old Order Amish."

On a crisp sixty-degree September morning, Verna and I sat on a sofa inside her home.

Verna, bubbly and cheerful, frequently looked down at her chubby-cheeked year-old daughter playing contentedly on the floor. Colorful toys scattered around the room. Her daughter's baby-fine blond hair was gathered atop her head and secured with a rubber band. She looked like a pixie.

"Tell me more about your life," I urged brown-haired, youthful Verna.

"I turned eighteen in October and left the following February. There were seven of us kids: five girls and two boys. We had running water, showers, bathtub, a water heater," she said reclining back on the sofa. "It was typical for our settlement."

"Wow, you were pretty modern for Amish." I reached down to tickle her little offspring who looked up and rewarded me with a toothless grin.

"We were higher than Swartzies. Between them and us were the Abe Troyer Amish. The Tobe Amish are higher than our Old Order. Down in Holmes County there are so many types of Amish. Our buggies had tape reflectors, a triangle, and lights on the side of the buggy." Her daughter crawled to the sofa. Verna picked her up and continued, "We had a 'stormfront'—"

"Whoa, what's that?" I interrupted. "I've not heard that word."

"It's a clear fiberglass-type flap that you could put down during rain and lift up in the summer. It wasn't allowed. But those who had one, put it down mainly 'for show.' When you're sixteen and not yet a member of the Church, that's another thing you do as a sign of being rebellious." Her cheeks lifted and eyes narrowed as she laughed.

This new information fascinated me – as a mom, a writer, her friend, and as an ever inquisitive learner. I watched her little pixie amuse herself rolling on the sofa with Mom. "What other things did the Amish teens do as disobedience?"

Still amused, "I got a camera when I was Amish. We weren't allowed music. My brother had a stereo. We weren't allowed electricity so he hooked his speakers to a twelve-volt battery." She smiled at her memory. "My brother hid all his things in the back of his buggy in a box under lock and key." She hopped up and put her daughter back on the floor, "I've got some pictures of my home and family," and dashed out of the room.

While she was absent, I thought of the rule-breaking stories Mosie, Harvey, Josh, Monroe and others laughed about. *Sarah hiding English clothes in the family attic.* I quietly mused, *there seems to be an Amish under belly of hiding prohibited goods. Rebellion. Gossip. Pushing the envelope. Then boasting about it to peers, while trying to avoid Church discipline. It could be typical adolescent behaviors in any culture.* I've met adults – Church members – who still do these things.

Verna returned hugging a scrapbook. She joined me on the sofa. Opened her treasured album and pointed to snapshots. "You've really kept this well maintained," I patted her shoulder. We flipped more pages. Looked at each picture. She stopped, pointed out the two-story, plain house where she lived, and her brother's buggy with the stormfront.

"I see your Order wore suspenders," I said pointing to one photo of an Amish lad.

"That's one of my younger brothers. Boys wear suspenders 'til they're fourteen. Then they don't."

"So you could tell the approximate age of a male by looking at his getup," I observed.

She nodded in agreement and turned the page. Verna showed me pictures of her Amish sisters, and scenic countryside. "I loved living out in the country. It was so beautiful."

"Why'd you leave?" I asked, curious to learn her reasons.

She closed her scrapbook. "I didn't like anything about Amish. My life was crazy. Dad left us when I was fifteen—he was an alcoholic. When I was six he started on the drugs. I remember a lot of it, like one night Dad came home drunk. Mom and Dad didn't yell but they raised their voices that night. Mom took his coat and threw it down the basement stairs 'cause it reeked of alcohol. I was awake and heard everything." She pulled her daughter to her lap and continued, "People knew he had an alcohol and drug problem. They treated him wrong. He lives in Columbus."

"Do you see him?"

"Oh yes, now we get along fine. But as a child, we fought. I'd get depressed and suicidal. I didn't have a lot of friends. I put on weight." She explained that her Amish settlement looked down on them. *Her life was chaotic,* I thought. "I felt like my family was always judged because of my dad. They decided to put me on medication."

"Who is 'they'?"

"The people. Even my grandfather told my mom I needed medication. She didn't agree."

"So why didn't she just tell them she wouldn't do it?" I asked. *All parents need to advocate for their child.* "I'm sorry at how you were labeled."

"I was in and out of a mental hospital from the time I was thirteen. It wasn't my or my mother's choice. The Amish mental hospital in Indiana . . . really messed up." She gave a stilted laugh and I wondered how much emotional pain she held back. From thirteen to nineteen—her entire adolescent years—Verna existed on a cocktail of medications.

"I've learned there are Amish doctors and dentists. What's the mental hospital like?"

"Amish work there—with nothin' more than eighth grade education. They feel they're educated 'nough and wanna help," answered Verna.

"Did you have counselors?" I was fishing to see if somebody was trained in mental health or social work.

"Yea, Amish ones. And the house parents made sure you got your medications. It was run by Amish . . . and some Mennonites. I've no doubt the medications messed me up."

I'd been a chaplain in a psychiatric facility. I knew some drugs build up to toxic levels and, there are contraindications of mixing chemicals in the body. "Did you have follow-up care with blood tests?"

"No." I twisted my mouth. My eyes blinked hard betraying my inner disbelief.

Hoping to help Verna know she wasn't the only one relegated to such a place, I added, "Marvin's parents made him go to one when they found out he wanted to leave. They told the staff to give him 'medication to change his mind,'" This flippant—and unethical—practice on children astounded and aggravated me.

She nodded as if to relate. "There's four I know of: Ohio, Indiana, Pennsylvania and Michigan."

"How do people find out about these Amish mental hospitals?"

"Oh word gets out." She rolled her eyes. "The Amish is one of the biggest gossip communities. If you want people to know something, you tell them and say, 'Now don't tell anyone.'" She giggled. "There was an English medical doctor who came and brought medications to the one I was in."

I bristled. Felt my heart pound harder. "You mean a licensed doctor brings medication into an unlicensed hospital and lets unlicensed staff dispense? That's illegal!" I exclaimed, wondering if they were using drugs in coercive practices like sedated submission. The *Diagnostic and Statistical Manual of Mental Disorders* (DSM) is the standard classification of mental disorders used by United States' mental health professionals. *Wonder if there was a DSM at these Amish mental hospitals or if they had a Pharmaceutical License to dispense.* Turning my thoughts back to Verna, I asked, "So what happened on the night you left?"

"The February night I left . . . my dad kicked me outta the house," she answered.

Confused by Verna's answer I asked, "But you wanted to leave anyway, right?"

"I was eighteen. Dad and Mom were divorced but he was visiting that night. Mom was on the verge of being put in the *bann* because of my rebellious behavior. She told Dad and then he told me I had a week to get outta the house—"

Bewildered, I interrupted, "Why would your mom be put in the *bann* because of you?"

She shook her head. Wrinkled her mouth. A smug look of insider-information. "That's how much control the Amish have." I must've looked doubtful because she continued, "I was going against everything Mom told me. I'd turn on my radio, party at English friends' homes. Hang out with kids who drove cars. I'd wear English clothes even though I was Amish." She looked at her daughter then turned to me, "I left *that* evening in three inches of snow."

My mom heart wanted to cradle the little Amish girl inside Verna.

She explained how her neighbor picked her up in his truck and dropped her at a friend's house. "I didn't know what to do. All I could think was I wanted to die. My life was messed up. It was crazy. My friend nervously phoned the police, believing I was gonna kill myself that night. When the cops came they talked me into releasing a knife I had in my hand."

"What happened then?"

"They took me to a mental hospital run by English. They had me under suicide watch for the first three days. I stayed about two weeks. That was a good thing," she paused with thought and smiled. "It gave me time to focus and plan what I'd do. They helped me 'regroup.'" She paused. Little pixie began to fuss and rub her eyes. Verna picked her up. "I'm going to lay her down for a nap." She left me alone.

I heard soothing words coming from the other room. Then quiet. Verna returned. She sat down and continued with her story. I learned that in those weeks under professional mental health care, her mom brought Verna's birth certificate, purse, English clothes, social security card—everything Verna needed to live on the outside. She'd always been warned about the worldly English; now she had to live in it.

"After they released me from that hospital," she said, "I lived with another ex-Amish for about two months. I got off my medications, lost weight, and my skin color improved." She jumped up, "Want to see a picture of me then?"

I watched Verna cross the room to a framed photograph. "See how ashen, how swollen my face was? It was because of all the medicines." *Cocktail of chemicals.* "Then I decided to live with my dad. He wanted me there."

I hung onto her word "wanted" and I hurt for her. "Your dad? Who kicked you out? The alcoholic and drug addict? Wanted you with him?" I knew the father/daughter bond can be strong but, I didn't get this paradox.

She sat down again. "Yea, I know. After I lived with him, it opened my eyes. I got to know him in a new way. It made me realize his life isn't the easiest either. Now I'll talk to him and we have a decent relationship." Verna smiled. "You want some water?"

"No thanks."

She inhaled deep. Sunk into the sofa. Laughed as she exhaled. "My mom and I have a better relationship now that I'm English. I have the best relationship with my whole family." She waited, then added, "I have more respect for them and they respect me now."

"You're blessed. Most of the ex-Amish I know are shunned, or they were at first. At best, their family relationships are strained."

She shook her head in acknowledgement. Hurried to add, "For a lot of 'em, when you're Amish they treat you like crap but when you leave they're friendly and want you to come back." She remembered an Amish woman who offered her a place to live if Verna returned to Amish. "Then there are those who shun you. The Amish are complex."

I learned that a year after Verna left, she moved in with a former Amish family. They introduced her to David, who'd just left the Amish. David and Verna spent time together talking. Exchanging stories. She said that an Amish minister called David to woo him back with promises of a newly built house. *Wonder where the minister got a phone?* Meanwhile, David's dad sent word to him that he wanted nothing to do with him since leaving the Amish.

Verna said that David was kind to her. A good listener. Handsome. Smart. They began dating. And during that time she tenaciously weaned herself off all the medications. Whatever they were.

"Since I'm off the medications," she smiled with raised eyebrows, "I don't get mad or have suicidal thoughts." Her voice wounded resolute. She paused. Smiled. Brightened.

I relished my time with my friend but, didn't want to prevent her from home responsibilities. I checked my watch. *We talked nearly two hours.* Verna reclined on the sofa. "You're tired, aren't you? Sorry if I strained your brain." *Lord, give her messages of worth and approval,* I prayed.

"Oh, it's okay. I'm just doing laundry today." She giggled and shrugged her shoulders.

"And being a mom. That's a fulltime job," I emphasized, reflecting her lightheartedness. I stood to leave, grabbed the keys out of my purse.

"Thanks for coming over. Fun talking to you," she said, followed by a long hug.

I stopped at the door. We hurriedly swapped some food recipes. I learned that Verna adores the canning and work ethic her mother taught her, and offered, "I'll bring you and David a bag of beans from our over-producing plants."

The young couple and their healthy one-year-old daughter remain connected to the Amish heritage by visiting her family. She frequently said, "David's calm and good to me. Good for me." Buoyant. Forgiving. Positive.

Nurturing. That's the Verna I know.

I left that day amused at an irony. David and Verna attend an independent house of worship called Overcomers Church.

"Nothing is better for self-esteem than survival." ~ Martha Gellhorn

Chapter 7

Marvin

"I'm driving to pick up another Amish," Uriah told me on the phone.

"Who is it?" I hear background road noise.

"Marvin. He's Old Order in Pennsylvania. Maybe if there's time, I'll bring him by your home."

The next Sunday morning, Marvin walked into our kitchen through the side door. Blue-jean clad, I looked at his youthful, clean face. Hair already shorn. Slender body. Eighteen years young. He'd just left his settlement.

Uriah brought him to meet my husband and me, and to visit our church. The congregation was used to meeting the former Amish who'd passed through my life.

When we walked into church, Marvin and Uriah scanned the foyer. Immediately our friends extended a hand to shake theirs, "Great to see you and thanks for visiting." A few asked generic questions. Marvin smiled. Shadowed me in the unfamiliar English church.

After service, we decided to eat lunch at Lynsey and Harvey's home – our daughter and son-in-law. Husband, Uriah, Marvin, and I loaded in my car. On the way, we stopped at a local grocery store for extra lunch food. I'll wait in the car," I said.

"Me too," added Marvin.

We sat in the enclosed silence. I in the front, Marvin in the back. I could hear him tapping on his cell phone. Not surprised that he'd already acquired the "worldly" convenience, I waited and wondered about this new lad in my vehicle.

I broke the calm, "Tell me about your parents." Street traffic passed.

"They made me go to a mental hospital."

"What?" I turned around to look at him in the back seat.

"When they found out I wanted to leave, they made me go to a mental hospital and told the doctors, 'Give him medicine to change his mind.'"

Silence again. He on his phone. I, letting this information – this boy's experience – sink in. Such a misunderstanding of a teenager's need for independence. Such a glib attitude toward psychiatric professionals.

"How'd they make you go?" I wondered aloud.

From the back seat, Marvin answered matter-of-factly, "They hired an

English driver to get me in the car."

I hesitated but, my curiosity about his mental hospital incident forced the question, "What was that like?"

"I didn't care," he snickered, "got to wear English clothes and watch TV . . . in bed. When my parents came to visit me, they got mad at the doctors for letting me wear English clothes. So from then on, I'd put on Amish clothes only when they'd visit."

"Where was the hospital?"

"Ohio."

"Was it a real one or an Amish one?"

"It was a real one."

"So did the doctors give you medicine?" I asked hoping it not true.

"Nah, they said I was normal."

"So obviously you didn't stay Amish," I quipped.

"Yah, my family watched me pretty close after I was discharged. But I still ran away." He tapped on his phone.

I was amused at how Marvin minimized the situation. No resentfulness in his tone. No anger. Just his reality. He didn't sound disgruntled, as I've heard some people accuse those who left Amish.

Marvin liberally shared his history, life on his farm, and reasons for leaving the Amish. He laughed. *He's more transparent than the others*, I thought. Soft-spoken, pensive, responsive, and gentle. Openness uncommon with most of the others I knew.

I shared about our Mosie, his cousin Levi, our son-in-law Harvey, and his cousin Josh, and named other former Amish God brought to my dinner table: Rudy, Noah, Andy, Uriah, and Dan. "They're great. I love them all. They've told me funny stories, and taught me a lot about their Amish upbringing." I paused to think how each had his own personality and needs – challenges. Remembered the time Rudy sat on my family room sofa and mourned, "Wish I had English parents," after he learned we were Mosie's English parents.

Suddenly Marvin declared, "You're like a mom to the ex-Amish."

Hmm, never seen myself that way. I just responded to a need – if I could. A meal. A hug. An invitation to watch TV. My insides tingled at Marvin's perception, and title. I smiled. Waited.

In the distance, I heard voices. They grew louder. The car doors opened and my husband and Uriah tossed in a sack of food. We continued our drive to Lynsey's home.

Through my experiences with other former Amish, I learned that they love playing games and teasing, and they all seem related or at least know each other. After lunch, we played a card game, teased, laughed. I mentioned the PBS TV documentary, *The Amish*, was airing in a week. Uriah, Marvin, Lynsey and Harvey agreed to come over and watch it with us. "I met the producer and film crew while they were filming in Ohio," I said, thinking, *it'll be interesting to see what scenes made it and what hit the cutting room floor.*

A week later, the guys arrived on a cool March evening in 2012. I tingled with excitement to host former Amish and to see the show because Levi was featured, and my husband and I were in one scene. Uriah and Marvin brought John – another young Old Order Amish who'd just left weeks prior.

"Here ya go," I handed popcorn and cold beverages to my guests. It seemed that all the Amish I knew ate popcorn like a staple. Blue jeans, big belt buckles and cowboy hats atop long-lost Amish haircuts covered our family room floor. I'd raised two daughters. This room full of boys – "sons" – made me feel inexperienced.

To add to the "educational" tone, I'd invited our minister. He'd told me that he wanted to learn more about these young men and the life they'd left. That night made the perfect, casual opportunity.

We watched, laughed, and learned. Seeing a documentary about Amish - with formers - is enlightening, exciting, and fun. One would pick out minor details to explain. Another would pipe up, "Yah, that's right," or "We didn't do that."

Moments of engaged silence were punctuated by humorous comments. In one scene, a flock of geese flew across the sky with singing in the background. Straight-faced Josh quipped, "We never had geese that sang." If they mourned the loss of their previous life, none showed it.

When the show ended, I gathered up empty popcorn bowls and bottles. Our minister casually asked one a question. Then another. Then conversation took over with the guys sharing stories of growing up Amish.

At ten o'clock that night, they pulled on their cowboy boots, donned their hats, and bid goodnight. I hugged each – John, Uriah, Josh, Marvin, and of course our son-in-law Harvey.

A new learning curve just launched for me.

One week later – to the day – Lynsey's text broke my morning routine, "Marvin's been in a bad accident. John's dead."

I felt an empty hole in my gut like a horse had kicked me. "What?" I texted back. "Call me!"

Lynsey and I chatted on the phone. She told me as much as she knew from Harvey. "How'd he know so soon and this much?" I asked.

"He got a text from another ex-Amish man."

Lynsey and I made hasty arrangements to rush to the hospital where Marvin had been taken. I didn't want Marvin to feel abandoned. Alone. While waiting for her to pick me up, I phoned the hospital to gather as much information as I could. His condition. His need for a parental figure. "Is anyone there with him?" I asked.

"Not yet."

I prayed during our two-hour-long drive to the trauma hospital. *Poor kid,* I thought, *only eighteen, no family support. So new and few friends.* My heart was heavy. *Marvin and John were just in my home!* So young. John's gone. Forever. I'd never see his face again nor get to know him. *Why God?*

We pulled into the Emergency Department lot, parked, and ran inside. There, the staff gave me grave information – as much as allowed. Lynsey and I sunk down in waiting room chairs. Waited. Marvin was being transported from the ED to the Critical Care Unit. The staff told me that I could be with him once they'd settled him in a bed.

The two of us paused a few more minutes, still reeling from the sudden shock and the long drive. A young ex-Amish couple walked in followed by a short, older man who'd been raised but left Old Order. I knew all three. The older man and I shared a similar passion for helping ex-Amish. He'd talked to Marvin over the phone while Marvin lived in Pennsylvania. But the two had never met.

I was elated to see more support for our young patient and hugged all three. Older Man tensed, unlike other times. *Was he annoyed at this interruption in his busyness?* He stood unbending. When I backed away he shot me dagger eyes. My mind contorted. *Was he surprised by my presence?* He knew Marvin and I had a connection, that Marvin visited our church and spent an afternoon with us. That he had come to our home to watch the PBS TV special. *Whatever!*

Lynsey and I, along with the three ex-Amish, climbed in the elevator to leave the ED. The other two shared snippets of the horrific car accident. Older Man unspeaking, was preoccupied with his phone. We rode up to the CCU and exited the elevator.

I introduced myself to the nurses, and explained that I wanted to "be there" for Marvin. They ushered me into his room. On crisp white linens laid a slender, bruised, bandaged, and nearly unconscious eighteen-year-old. A cervical collar around his neck prevented him from turning his head in my direction. "Hi Marvin," I whispered. His eyes rolled to meet mine. He managed a feeble smile of relief at my presence.

Reaching out his hand, Marvin gripped mine. He squeezed tight. "Don't let my parents know because they'll say this is my punishment for leaving Amish." His voice limp. Then he grimaced in discomfort.

In a nanosecond, I sensed his emotional agony mingled with physical injury and pain. He looked up at the nurses, scurrying around for vitals and med checks and, claimed, "This is my mom."

Oh, if I could really be his mom. I'd hug him. Soothe him. He'd relax knowing I had only his best interest in mind. In hushed voices the nurses and the surgeon discussed his care plan. Then one summoned a social worker, and another said, "Call the OR."

The nurses and surgeon had assessed Marvin. Spinal fracture of C2 and C3, broken hip, right arm, and left femur. Smashed elbow. Crushed pelvis. Multiple sprains, cuts, and contusions. Lung puncture. Surgery was imminent.

Lynsey joined us. Then Older Man slipped in and stood bedside. He introduced himself to Marvin. "Oh, okay," said Marvin, "nice to meet you."

While they exchanged a few words, I crept over to the nurses and whispered, "I'm not really his mom. He just left the Amish and has no family, so he attached to me." I felt sensitive to Marvin's dignity, and didn't want to contradict his frame of mind.

In the craziness, I asked Lynsey, "What's that for?" pointing to the wires, cords, and IV's enveloping Marvin's body. Having worked in an ED, she knew what the monitors meant. She was my education. My comfort. "Thanks for her, God," I silently prayed.

The neurosurgeon began explaining the imperative surgery to Marvin, looking at both of us. Being ex-Amish and English-language limited, I saw Marvin's blank stare. The words were puzzling. I sensed he was muddled.

"Can you explain this in laymen language?" I asked the surgeon. He paused, smiled, and resumed his description in simpler terms.

"Any questions?" He looked at me and then Lynsey. We understood and indicated no questions with a shake of our heads. Older Man maintained his station by Marvin, head downward and motionless. To confirm, the surgeon asked, "Marvin, do you understand what's going to happen to fix your body?"

"Yes," he said as he slightly nodded in acknowledgment.

Some uneasiness left me as Marvin appeared to absorb his initial treatment plan. Lynsey looked down at him functioning on pain meds. Traumatized. Helpless. A picture of her former patients. I sensed God's confirmation that we were in the right place, at the right time.

"This is going to be delicate," continued the surgeon, "We may forego the neck surgery and implant a medical halo to restrain his neck and head. "We need a Medical Power of Attorney (POA) due to the seriousness of the situation." He continued, "Marvin may need decisions made in his behalf while unconscious."

"Fine," I said. "It's Marvin's decision. He may want this other ex-Amish man to speak for him . . . or Lynsey." I looked at both with begging eyes. Knowing the gravity – the potential obligation – of being a POA, I wanted Marvin to feel comfortable with his choice.

We left; Lynsey, me, the older man. Stood near the nurses' station as the thick curtain encircled Marvin's room. His nurses, the hospital social worker, and surgeon privately and quietly discussed the matter.

Looking at Older Man I commented, "I'm glad the surgeon explained things to Marvin in a way he could understand."

"He doesn't need your help. I just let the ex-Amish fall down and they learn from that," he snapped. His hostility stung.

"But, everyone needs help understanding medical procedures. Especially those out of a culture that isn't as skilled in our language." I waited for his response. Nothing. "You mad at me about something?"

He looked away and mumbled, "Let's just see who Marvin wants. It's his choice."

Minutes later, a nurse poked her head from behind the curtain. "He wants you," she said looking at me.

I loved this adolescent. What a heavy responsibility to be his "voice." Older Man glared at me, his eyes white-hot. He turned away tapping on his cell phone, and headed toward the hospital's waiting area.

I watched as the medical team quickly whisked Marvin to the OR. The sound of his heart monitor fading. Gone. Then Lynsey and I rejoined the other three and waited . . . during the predicted three-hour surgery. We prayed together. Then independently. "I'm glad he chose you to be his POA," piped up the young ex-Amish gal. A smile slid across her face. Older Man tapped on his cell phone. Stood up, moved out of hearing range, and murmured in the mouthpiece.

Lynsey and I addressed the other two, "You know any details?" The male had arrived on the ugly crash scene seconds before first responders. He told us that Marvin was riding in the back seat of a car driven by ex-Amish John. The guys were zipping along a two-lane road on their way to work that morning. John lost control, slid, and careened onto a lawn. His car slammed into a tree, rebounded, flipped midair, tossed John from the driver's seat like a rag doll, twisted, and landed in a mangled heap. The violent noise stopped, with the front-seat occupant trapped by the misshapen metal. Marvin was rammed further back, where his head was pinned in the trunk.

Then the agonizing moans from the two survivors.

The shrill sound of sirens grew louder. Suffering in excruciating pain, eased faintly by the cold morning air, Marvin waited – conscious – while first responders feverishly worked ninety minutes to free him from the fatal carnage. They cradled his neck. Immobilized his broken limbs. Wiped off the blood. Dressed the open wounds. Loaded him in the awaiting ambulance for the nearest hospital. From there he was life-flighted to a trauma CCU two hours from our home.

The other injured lad, with broken ribs, was treated at the same hospital. His parents retrieved him and took him back to their Amish settlement.

Stunned by specifics of the horrific crash that seized the life of one, and injured two, I sat quiet. The older man returned, sat down. I tried to talk to him but his answers were terse or argumentative.

"Harvey and I have talked and he's welcome to live with us while he's recuperating," Lynsey offered up to the trio.

Meanwhile word of the accident reached Marvin's Amish parents because the older man announced, "They're on their way here now." I would later learn that they hired an English man to drive them to Ohio.

Oh boy, I wondered. How will they react? Will they be nice? Ignore me? Worried? Stoic? With this on my mind, I questioned if Lynsey and I should leave. Would it be helpful . . . or harmful . . . for his parents to be with Marvin? From what he'd shared with me, his parents were shunning him. So why would they come to the hospital?

A phone call to our waiting area interrupted my reflections. "He made it through surgery and is doing well," announced the surgeon. "He'll be back in his room soon."

I exhaled relief, turned and told the others. We glanced at each other relieved, and our moods lightened.

Two hours later, I spotted a black-garbed couple. The solemn man with his long peppered beard wore a black wool hat. The woman in her kapp and bonnet, shawl around her shoulders, and plain dress nearly touching her ankles walked behind the man. His parents. I smiled at them. They remained placid. I lingered in the waiting room while his parents visited their barely conscious boy. Every breath was a prayer. *Please help this visit be positive.* I didn't know what to do or say. I needed Divine guidance. Lynsey and I went down to the hospital cafeteria to grab a bite to eat. We sipped coffee and reviewed the day's maze of events.

The nurse paged me to his room after his parents left. "I had to tell them to leave. My priority is my patient."

"What do you mean?" I asked feeling puzzled by her comment.

"His heart monitor begin to raise. I went in his room and he pointed at his parents and indicated to me that he wanted them to leave!"

"Why?"

"Don't know but, he wanted them gone." She added, "When I told them, the dad tried to argue and resist me. Guess he didn't like taking orders from a woman." She grinned and resumed her paperwork.

Later, in the hallway, his Amish mother broke her silence, "Is he living with you?" Her eyes searching for information.

"No." I smiled.

"Then where?" Her concerned voice mixed with a tone of disapproval.

"Don't know. Somewhere in Ohio." I shrugged my shoulders. I wanted to talk and encourage another mom that her child would be well cared for but, she joined her husband as he walked down the hospital corridor.

Reassured that Marvin was recovering in his room, the other three ex-Amish announced, "We need to go." They'd faithfully remained at the hospital much of the day. The abrupt interruption in their morning upset their day. I understood they needed to resume their schedules. For me, flexibility. With no imminent writing deadlines, I could linger. Lynsey shadowed me back into Marvin's room.

"As his POA, you need to stay here or at least available until Marvin's fully conscious," one nurse called out to me. We were two hours from home. My husband was due for supper. I needed to call him. I needed to alert our church members to pray. And I wanted to cooperate with the hospital.

Lynsey remained with Marvin and I walked the ex-Amish trio to the visitor elevator. I would later phone my husband and close friends. Lynsey would make her connections. Suddenly, the elevator doors slid apart and Uriah exited. "Hi," I said happy to see reinforcement. Happy to see him again.

He neared me, planted himself a foot from my face and said, "I hear you're taking over."

"What?" I was taken back at his ambush.

"I hear you want to control everything." He eyed me sternly. Not like the easy-going lad who'd recently been in our church and my home.

"Who told you that? Nothing is further from the truth," I responded feeling a flush to my face. "My only goal is to be available if needed." I smiled to ease the tension.

"Well, I heard you want to be in charge," he persisted.

"Hey, if you want to be in charge – whatever that means – go for it. I'm not stopping you or anyone. Aren't we all here to support Marvin?" My eyes rolled in disbelief at the wild confrontation coming from this young man.

I'd learned that although Amish may prohibit cell phones, they network, and delight in settlement news. Many wallow in gossip. Allegations arise. If not restrained – or stopped – an innocent person is the target of rumors. Condemnation. *The look*. Many who leave the Amish, continue that imbedded behavior.

Stung from the false allegation – the suspicion – I accompanied the other three out of the hospital. *Maybe I'll get some comfort from them. Maybe they'd stop the rumor.*

Outside, in the parking lot, I leaned in the opened car window as the gal, her companion, and Older Man buckled seatbelts. "I'm sorry if it looks like I'm trying to take over. I'm just here to help Marvin." The older man scrutinized me. My eyes questioned. His chilled. They sped away.

Back in the CCU, the nursing staff updated Lynsey and me. They encouraged me to stay overnight and then made arrangements for on-site housing. Lynsey called off from work for the following day. I hadn't bargained for this – it mushroomed – neither did I begrudge it. I inhaled and exhaled prayers. Marvin needed calm and consistency.

"It's going to take him months if not a year to recover, Mom," Lynsey predicted.

After an exhausting day, and visiting hours ended, Lynsey and I said our goodbyes and headed to our awaiting overnight accommodation. I saw his parents walking to a nearby room. They chose to stay, too.

In the small and most welcomed room, Lynsey and I called our husbands. Recounted the accident to our friends and others who committed to pray. We munched on snacks and looked out the window across to the hospital. Lynsey eventually dozed off in her bed. I tossed. Dozed. Awoke. Imagined. Questioned. Replayed the denunciation of my motives. Couldn't sleep. Tried. My mind drifted to Marvin. *Was he awake? Asleep? In pain? How are his vitals?*

Dawn dimly lit our room when I looked at the clock. Four in the morning. I called the CCU, "Please," I pleaded, "may I come over and just sit in Marvin's room? I won't make a sound and I won't get in your way. He needs the comfort of a familiar face."

"Alright but, you must to be very quiet."

"I just want to be there in case he wakes up and needs something."

With her permission, I quickly, quietly dressed and crept out of the room as Lynsey slept.

Tiptoeing into the silent CCU, I located Marvin's primary nurse to escort me into his room. To my surprise, he was awake. "Hi Brenda," he mouthed. "My parents came."

"I know."

"Dad gave me *the look!*"

I knew what he meant. I'd learned from the others that Amish bestow *the look* – a glower – of condemnation and disapproval to members who misbehave. Those who leave get *the look.*

"Why would his parents shun him?" the nurse quietly asked me.

"Oh, it's complicated. They feel he's going to hell for leaving Amish."

Even with my experiences helping Mosie, Josh, and others, I felt overwhelmed by this novel and serious responsibility that Marvin and the staff placed on my shoulders. Awareness of the physical and emotional recovery facing this young man plagued my thoughts. My mind went back to my years working as a hospital chaplain. When patients were brutally injured they often suffered slow thinking. Roller-coaster emotions. Memory loss. Feelings of vulnerability. Survivor guilt and potential speech impairment from head wounds.

Seven in the morning, I phoned my husband. "I really need to get home today," I whispered into the receiver. "Need to rest and take care of some household business. His parents are here and other ex-Amish will come to see him." I hung up the phone and wondered where the older man was. Marvin looked up at the ceiling. Quiet.

Lynsey joined me and together we went down to the hospital cafeteria. As we scarfed a small breakfast, we reviewed the previous day's events, our overnight sleep – or lack of - and plans for that day. We made one last visit up to Marvin's room. He was alert. The intubation tube dangled from his throat and he wrestled against its intrusion. He struggled to speak so I handed him a pencil and pad, "Here Marvin, use this to talk."

"I want this tube out!" he scrawled with his uninjured arm.

"I know but, it must stay in until they remove it," Lynsey explained.

The tube pressed against his chapped lips revealing his toothless gums. I'd alerted the nurses before surgery that he had dentures. They stared in disbelief that a teen had a full set, and quickly removed them.

"What can I do to help?" I whispered to Marvin. He pointed to his cracked lips. I rubbed over them with a moisturizer.

My phone rang. On the other end was a former Amish who told me of his plans to stop in during his lunch hour. "Great," I replied, "I've got to go home, shower, see my husband, and eat."

I told Marvin of my plans and he scribbled with the pencil, "You coming back?"

"If you want me to."

He nodded a yes.

"I'll stay at home tonight and then tomorrow, come back up and stay overnight again." You need to rest because you'll have a noontime visitor.

Lynsey and I drove the two hours home exhausted. We needed to refresh and relax. But we knew we'd face oodles of texts and calls from concerned church friends.

At home, I relaxed with my husband. Thought of the household tasks to catch up on and calls yet to make. Mosie phoned. He knew the older man and those who'd been at the hospital. "I hear you're trying to run the show. And I'm hearing all kinds of bad things about you."

I gulped hard. Felt a tingling of nervousness. "Like what?"

"You're trying to control who visits Marvin and you want to run everything."

"Not true," I answered feeling both hurt and anger. "And why would you believe them, Mosie?" Blood pounded loud in my ears, my heart pierced from his doubt in me. "You should know me better than that."

"I don't know who to believe." His allegiance confused, he hung up the phone.

Tears welled up as I described the spiteful accusations to my husband. The growing hostility against me. "Where'd I go wrong?" I turned to my husband for comfort. An explanation. Anything.

"You've done nothing wrong except interfere with someone's lunge for control."

"I don't get it. The ninth commandment warns against bearing false witness."

"Yes, it's destructive. Someone is afraid, unwilling to trust you since you weren't Amish. They've rounded their wagons keeping you on the outside."

"But I've helped other former Amish. I don't get why this situation is creating chaos. To divert my mind, I went out shopping with a friend. Older Man texted, "Me and some friends are going to see Marvin tonight."

"Great." I replied to his message, "I'm at home."

"That's between God and Marvin."

I furrowed my forehead. Reread his last text. It made no sense. I showed it to my friend. It made no sense to her. It was like he had a text template ready to put me in my place. Went home and showed the enigmatic text to my husband. It made no sense to him.

Confused and annoyed and determined to thwart the attacks, I phoned my minister with an update. We made plans for me to ride up to the hospital with him and his wife the following afternoon. Then I could keep my promise to Marvin and stay another day with him.

It was day three following his accident when the three of us arrived.

Marvin was alert. His intubation tube had been removed and he sat up in the elevated bed. "Hello," he greeted our minister and his wife in a scratchy voice, a result of the tube.

I wanted to leave them alone in the room so they could have privacy and talk, so I turned to leave.

"Where you going?" stopped Marvin.

"Out in the hall. You'll be fine and I'll be back."

I waited in the hallway. Saw one of the ex-Amish who'd been with me the first day. He brought a friend. Older Man didn't accompany them. Hadn't seen him since that first day of the accident.

Raised eyebrows greeted me. "Lynsey just wants to take Marvin home to her house so she can make money from taking care of him," the male charged.

"What?" I gasped in disbelief. Lynsey and Harvey offered Marvin a home to recover in when the time came, and they hoped to ease his mind and assure him of friendship. They knew it'd be weeks before he could be transferred to a rehab center then cleared for home care. And with his serious injuries, the hospital would not dismiss him except to an assisted living situation. "Ridiculous! Lynsey won't make money off Marvin," I defended. "She and Harvey are being generous to offer him a place to recover. With his injuries, it'll take months."

"She's a nurse and she'll get *paid* for taking care of him, they say."

"Who's 'they'?"

"My sister."

Ludicrous. My patience was tested. I wondered. *There must be infected emotional wounds oozing antagonism.* "That's called a conflict of interest," I explained. "She cannot invite a friend to recover in her home and expect her job to pay her for it."

"Well, others want him to live with them."

"Fine. Do they know about occupational and respiratory therapy, caring for a halo in his skull? Potential infections—"

"They want him near this hospital and other ex-Amish," interrupted his companion.

"Harvey's ex-Amish!" *Were they ignoring that fact?* "He's conscious. I'm no longer the POA anyway. It's his decision." I shrugged my shoulders and started to walk away.

"And the gal who was here that first day said, 'the older man should've been his POA. Not you.'"

"Wait," I stopped and turned to face them. "At first she said that she was glad Marvin chose me."

They stared. Stolid. Their suspicion was closing down our relationship.

I calmed my growing exasperation. Phoned the gal who'd flip flopped, "Why'd you say that?"

"I got t'thinking 'bout it," and relayed her conversation with the older ex-Amish man. "On our drive home t'gether from t'hospital, he said that *he* should've been POA." She sounded embarrassed. Unwilling to trust her original support of me but instead rely on Older Man to tell her what to think. I'd learned years before that this culture is male-controlled.

"They have no relationship," I reasoned. "Why would Marvin appoint a practical stranger for such an obligation?" It was a no-win conversation. I ended my call and hung up the phone.

I felt a tap on my back and turned to face my minister. "We must go now," he stated. "We've prayed and visited with Marvin and, don't want to wear him out."

I watched the two walk down the hall toward the elevators. Felt like I'd lost sensible allies. I'd told my minister on the drive up about a negative spirit. He listened, offered his counsel, prayed with and for me. But he wasn't the one drowning in the cesspool of mounting rumors and ingratitude. They disappeared and I questioned myself for not going back with them. I collapsed in the chair by Marvin's bed and looked at him. So defenseless. Healing. He was peaceful. I mirrored him. Then my cell phone rang disturbing the calm. "We're coming to see Marvin," Mosie told me. His voice sounded resolute.

"Okay. Who is 'we'?" I asked guarded.

He named two former Amish guys plus himself. I sensed another confrontation. Through the years, my experience with this culture had taught me that Amish men group-confront an "unruly" person. I'd heard stories of the deacon and preachers together visiting a home to impart discipline. Although these were former Amish, they tended to behave in the familiar ways of their upbringing.

Minutes later I looked up. The three stood in the doorway to Marvin's room. Three young, robust men. *Were they acting on their own or also under the influence of the older man? His emissaries?*

Wait, I told myself, it's my choice to show grace. To be rational. To show them tolerance and charity.

The four of us left Marvin asleep and we sat in a corner of the waiting area. My heart thumped hard. I hoped they'd be respectful. *Lord, help me.* "So what's the problem with me being here with Marvin?" I broke the silence. Smiled. Tried to look relaxed.

"He needs to be allowed to make up his own mind. And they think you are trying to control him," started one former Amish.

"You talk about letting him choose then argue with his choice. That's control in disguise." *They wanted him to choose . . . their choice.* "Besides," I reminded my young hearers, "Marvin is still on high-powered drugs. He needs simple explanations, no pressure, and time to think. He may not know what he wants or who to live with when he's dismissed. His mind should be on recuperation not on conflicting messages."

"Yah," agreed another nodding his head – not Mosie. Ouch! That hurt.

We sat. Me in one chair. The three – opposite – facing me down. The trio took turns tag-teaming me with what they'd heard behind my back. Drilling me with rhetorical questions. Mosie stood. Paced. I wanted my husband. Lynsey. Harvey. Someone to bring rationality. Be on my side.

"Well, guys," I said in my most calm voice. "I'm just here to help. And Marvin can tell me to leave anytime he wants. He can do his months of rehab with anyone he chooses. He'll need help eating. Walking. Getting dressed. His body will demand physical and occupational therapy. Why can't all of us work together for his good?

The trio looked at me silently. Then they headed towards Marvin's room. I sat alone and waited until they were finished with him and walked past me on their way to the visitor elevator. I felt like a flea-bitten, kicked mutt. Repugnant. Pushed away. I'd seen it in their faces. Felt it in their look. Heard it in their voices. My "son" Mosie drawn into the spirit of suspicion.

Back in Marvin's room I sat. Whipped. Listened to the voices in the hall. Listened to the beep of his heart monitor. Revisited the times the older man slipped in after I'd left – told he avoided me.

Is it my imagination? Did I rush in where angels fear to tread? I tried to sleep. To rest my soul. A blanket of condemnation fell over me. Suffocated me. *I'll leave. No, I'll stay.* The haunting voice whispered in my ear, "You're unwanted." I prayed to God. My prayer seemed smothered. Took a deep breath. Exhaled slowly. Prayed for Marvin, *please don't let this slow his recovery.* I tried to focus on God and His goodness. If I left who'd be here for Marvin? Older Man had other demands on his time and attention. My husband and Lynsey, at their jobs. My minister, needed elsewhere. *Why wasn't my support wanted? Was it because I was English? A woman? Jealous opposition?*

I needed someone to defend me and my caring motives. The nurse came in the room. Checked Marvin's vitals. Saw my tears. I looked away. She recorded notes in his chart and left.

I don't have to take this. Let someone else. I caved in. I couldn't stay the night. Phoned my husband at work, "You've got to come get me. I need to come home *now*."

"What's wrong?" his voice concerned. Wanting me.

"I'll tell you later. Just come get me."

Immediately, the internal battle eased. Gathering up my coat, purse, and books I'd brought to pass the time, I stood by Marvin's bed. He opened his eyes and looked up at me. I felt warm tears roll down my cheek. "I love you but I have to leave. I'm not wanted here."

"I know. I'm sorry for you. You're a nice lady." His eyes watched mine.

"I'll leave and won't come back – not until you call and say you want me." I wiped away tears, tried to hold back. Chin quivering, "I know some people are telling you that I'm trying to control you."

"Yah," he acknowledged. "I know." His eyes confirmed my fear.

"So if I leave son, that'll prove it's an irrational accusation. Leaving may calm down the situation so you can focus on you and getting well." I felt indignant for Marvin. Others were troubling him with false allegations, planting seeds of uncertainty. That wasn't love for him. That was their selfishness.

I left his room and walked down the corridor to wait in the lobby. After an hour my husband met me near the hospital's entrance. We walked to his truck. Tears spilled out my eyes. I was hungry. Felt betrayed. Misunderstood. Worthless.

On the drive home, my husband asked about Marvin. "He's doing better," and I shared his progress. Tears flowed as I relayed my challenging day and then thought, *Satan wants to cause havoc where there could be harmony. I could still pray for Marvin.* I comforted myself. *Relay his progress to praying friends.*

Marvin and I kept in touch by phone. He texted. Messaged me on social media when he was strong – and bored. He told me when he was being transferred out of CCU and to a new rehab facility. "Come see me," he invited.

"I felt pushed away," I replied.

"*I* never pushed you away!"

For weeks, I cowered in my home like a beaten dog. Licking my wounds. Hurt. Cross. Confused. I called and talked to Mosie in an attempt to alter his misguided thoughts and mend our weakened relationship.

In my defense, my good and wise husband phoned the older ex-Amish man. "Brenda was just trying to help," he explained. "She had the flexible time to be with him bedside, and be his moral support."

"I felt like a third wheel," he justified in a loud and militant voice.

"I think we should discuss this."

"I think we should just part ways," he ended.

Months passed. I was still struggling to understand, forgive. To show grace to my accusers. A few from that ex-Amish cluster never spoke to me again. I didn't dislike Older Man just lost respect for him. Prayed that I could recognize and resist being used for evil. To be tolerant of those who were lost on their path. Prayed they would find guidance.

Six months later, Marvin phoned. His voice strong. Optimistic. "Got that halo taken off," he said. "I'm walking by myself. Got a good place to live where they're nice. Still seeing my doctors. I can't extend my arm because of my elbow. The doctor said that it'll eventually get straight." *Praise God*, I cheered.

Within our family, we lightened the load of those ugly accusations when one of us would make a comment, another would randomly quip, "That's between God and Marvin." It made no sense but the humor helped in the healing.

A year later, Marvin drove down to see me, my husband, Lynsey and Harvey. He met me in our church foyer. We hugged. He looked different, a bit frail. Walked with a limp. He'd regained his independence. Was working and studying for his GED. "I want to go into the National Guard," he announced.

"You know you're a walking miracle," I said, relieved that the year was over . . . for both of us. I thought about the things he'd shared with me before and after his accident. He told me of his memories of the wreck. His perceptions. His healing. And his growth toward God.

Three years later, we sat together in my family room. I needed to revisit the mess. I clarified why I had to leave the hospital that day. Marvin slowly nodded his head. In his soft, soothing – almost sad – voice he said, "When I was Amish there were lots of times I was made to feel guilty and blamed for things I didn't do."

I had thought long about why God allowed this mess. The negative feelings. The broken relationships. The slander, entitlement, anger, jealousy, and manipulation.

Then, I finally got it. *Glad God is patient with me.* I accepted the rare gift He had given me three years ago. The ugliness and my pain were God's gifts. He gave me opportunity to experience a side of life for many Amish. Regulated, and suspected, and doubted, and falsely blamed. Our minister said in a sermon, "Suspicion is an expression of rejection." I *felt* the agonized rejection of "my" kids who escaped the condemnation. Their God-given spirit must have cried out, *I quit. I give up. I don't have to take this.*

I saw an underground stream of control roaring deep below the peaceful, romanticized image. My wounds led to wisdom. Now I can share more awareness, compassion, and sensitivity to those who choose to leave their Amish life.

"Praise You for Your sovereignty over the broad events of my life and over
the details.
With You, nothing is accidental, nothing is incidental, and no experience is
wasted. You hold in Your own power my breath of life and all my destiny.
And every trial that You allow to happen
is a platform on which You reveal Yourself, showing Your love and power,
both to me and to others looking on.
Thank You that I can move into the future non-defensively, with hands
outstretched to whatever lies ahead, for You hold the future and You will
always be with me, even to my old age . . .
and through all eternity."

Ruth Myers, *Thirty-One Days of Praise*

Appendices

Appendices

A.
Resources for Further Reading

To broaden your knowledge about the Amish, check out these non-fiction books:

Speaking Amish: A Beginner's Introduction to Pennsylvania German, by Lillian Stoltzfus / www.speakingamish.com

Plain Secrets: An Outsider among the Amish, by Joe Mackall

Unser Leit . . . The Story of the Amish, by Leroy Beachy

Amish Deception: An Autobiography, by David E. Yoder

An Amish Journey to Forgiveness: Discovering My Anabaptist Roots and Destiny, by Ben Girod

And these websites:

Amish Deception, www.amishdeception.com.

Beyond Buggies & Bonnets, www.BrendaNixonOnAmish.blogspot.com.

Amish Beliefs and Practices http://christianity.about.com/od/Amish-Religion/a/Amish-Beliefs.htm.

Escaping the Amish,

www.fourhourworkweek.com/blog search Escaping the Amish.

B.
Amish Parents' Letter to "Wayward" Child

Desperate for their child's return and convinced their child has no hope on the outside, Amish parents often send a letter. I've read various versions. Below is an excerpt from the letter Mosie's parents gave him when he briefly visited his family farm:

> There must be no looking back with a lingering longing look upon Sodom. Get thee out hence. "The reason I am writing to you is my wife and I were with the Beachy Mennonite Church for about twenty years. And it was also very hard on my dear father and mother when we left the Amish Gma. They came to visit us soon after and admonished us out of love, and asked us to come back. But we hardened our hearts against parental instruction and against conviction. . . .Yes, I knew I was living in sin by not obeying my parents. I knew I was breaking God's command, and I knew I was condemned. After several years my mother became sick and died. She went down into her grave broken-hearted. Some years later my dear father also died and went into his grave broken-hearted. . . . Finally the dear Lord gave us grace to come back and live our VOWS. Before he died I promised my father we want to repent and come back to the Amish church. That gave him some consolation. . . . This was very hard on our pride, to come back to the Amish church and give up our nice cars, tractors, and electricity, and confess that we went the wrong direction. . . . Now I would like to admonish you dear Brother and Sister out of love for Christ's sake. How vast important the command is to honor father and mother. . . . The authority of parental instruction is repeated over and over again throughout God's mighty looking glass. God never intended young people to be independent of their parents. . . . I am pained continually and feel sorry for young folks who rise up against their parents in disobedience and join a more

liberal church. . . . Oh, dear children take warning, deal faithfully with your own soul, do it now. . . . Just think what a great debt we owe to our Christian parents! Be warned, remember children, the way to Heaven is paved with obedience, and the way to Hell is paved with disobedience."

Monroe ran up to me one day and tossed this letter in my direction. I didn't know what it was until I opened the envelope. It was from his parents. Part of the letter read:

> Please do not miss treat your parents and make them so betrubt [miserable]. Please do not keep them so awake during the night of fear that you children may go to hell. And for them to think if they don't try to help youns that they may have to give count for youns children. I take hell like it may be like a pool or lake of pitch or fire and like a smell of sulphur burning. So that you can't hardly stand the smell. And the eyes would so burn and water, and like worms would be gnawing on the body. And would be so crying that the teeth would clapper. So children think twice what you do if you don't obey The Parents.

A former Old Order Amish told this story:

> I read letters to a son from his mother. The son had moved out of the house and the parents were heartbroken. The family sent letter after letter begging him to come home. If he would only give up his wicked lifestyle, they had plenty of room for him at home. The letters were heartbreaking, but the son stayed away. He knew he couldn't go home because his 'sinful' lifestyle was simply this: he wanted to stop being Amish and live a faith-based Christian life.

C.
Catching the Fence Jumpers: How You Can Help

"Brenda, how can I help ex-Amish adjust?"

I'm often asked about the needs of former Amish or ways to help them adjust to life on the outside. Some people think ex-Amish are like anyone else – nothing is farther from the truth. Most people cannot grasp the myriad and basic needs of these precious young adults.

Those of us who are friends with formers feel endeared to them. We might teasingly call them "Fence Jumpers" and I look at myself as one with outstretched arms ready to catch and soften their landing.

In my experience, there is one of three main reasons an Amish person leaves; to escape the rigid, oppressive rules; to explore religious freedom and live a faith-based life; or simply to shed the Amish life and work and live elsewhere. I could go into detail and share stories about each of these three reasons but, that's another book. To keep it focused, I'll answer the question of helping.

Since I live with, love, and assist Swartzentruber and conservative Old Order people, my answers apply to these two affiliations:

1) Recognize they grew up speaking Deutsch; therefore **they're ESL or ESOL** - an educator's term for English as a Second Language or English for Speakers of Other Languages. There are many of our words they don't understand, weren't introduced to, nor comprehend. When talking to ex-Amish, watch for subtle facial cues that they don't understand a word, then explain or define it. You don't need to "dumb down" your language but do bear in mind and respect that they need some comprehension help and typically won't ask you to explain. **Love looks out for the needs of others. It does not boast. It is not proud.**

I've found that common words - mayhem, astronaut, summary - are unfamiliar to many ex-Amish. Respect their dignity and need to learn, be empathetic, alert, and explain words.

2) Offer to help the ex-Amish obtain a birth certificate and/or a social security number. The ones I know left without a birth certificate . . .

to our government, they were nonexistent. Since most Amish do home-births, parents may forgo filing a birth certificate. This was the case of Monroe and Josh. In these cases, the individual must go to the county seat of their birth, and pay for a new birth certificate. This may be an arduous and time-consuming process. A Swartzentruber Amish man phoned me once asking if I could help his wife get her birth certificate. It seems she was born at home, in another state, and her mother never filed a birth certificate. The gal was now married and living in Ohio without any records. We had to contact her birth state, gather affidavits from the Amish relatives present at the birth - who'd be willing to sign an affidavit - and wait. If you've ever waded through legal paperwork you can appreciate the needed patience and diligence.

Likewise, applying for a social security number is a prerequisite for employment. It is illegal to hire anyone who doesn't have a social security number. Even if you want to serve former Amish, you do them no favor if you model breaking our laws.

3) Ask if he/she needs **clothing or housing**. Most of the ones I know left with two immediate goals: cut their hair and go to Walmart for English clothes. But, as you know, clothing isn't a one-time purchase; most will need a growing wardrobe. Since their clothing was always dictated and they had no freedom of choice, they may not know what they like or dislike. I found this true with Marvin when I bought a shirt for him. He was grateful then wasn't sure if he liked it or not. The bold colors and patterns were unfamiliar and counter-cultural. No offense was taken; it was just another move up the learning curve. A week later, Marvin told me he liked the shirt after two other teens said they liked it. I guess he needed some validation to his tastes.

4) Encourage them to **earn a GED**. I've repeatedly shared with Harvey, Mosie, Josh, and others, "I love you for who you are!" However, in our society, formal education is valued plus a GED testifies to self-discipline toward goal achievement. A GED will empower ex-Amish with confidence and new opportunities. The uphill struggle to earn this certification is exhausting due to their limited schooling. Although they completed Amish school at 8th grade, they never had homework and Amish teachers rarely have any credentials beyond 8th grade. In our GED programs, high school courses are taught to these ESL students with barely a middle-school education. Starting to see their struggle?

For those who aspire to go on to college, the Amish Descendant

Scholarship Fund, a non-profit program, provides financial assistance. You can help ex-Amish by donating to this worthy scholarship fund.

5) **Live graciously and give unconditional love.** "A loving heart is the beginning of all knowledge," observed Thomas Carlyle. Unconditional love is messy; it falls outside black/white lines, it isn't simple, is defined differently by each person, demands spiritual stamina, maturity, grit, and at times awkwardness. Besides that, it can drain you!

 I know one man who targets and attaches onto ex-Amish, beats them over the head with his King James Bible, pressures salvation, baptism, and church membership . . . in his church. Swartzentruber and conservative Old Order Amish grow up in a work-equals-worthy environment; they conform to this man's pressure only because they believe obedience to him is synonymous with salvation. Live graciously and love unconditionally. Let the Holy Spirit do *His job* of softening and preparing people's hearts for true repentance and salvation.

 I'm only one person—not a program or organization. I receive no pledges, donations, and volunteer workers. I'm willing to befriend those who, for one reason or another, left. Thank you for your prayers. Gratitude to many others who've also responded.

D.
Swartzentruber Ordnung

*Recollected by an Ohio Swartzentruber Church member
with commentary*

The German word "Ordnung" loosely translates to the English word "order." The Ordnung is an oral set of orders – or rules – kept and enforced by the bishop, preachers, and deacon. It's the Amish "blueprint" of expected behavior. Occasionally, the Ordnung is added to when particular needs and situations arise. These rules can change through the years.

One could spend a massive amount of time writing out the settlement's Ordnung but, here's the "Cliff's Notes." Twice a year, Swartzentrubers have Ordinance Church, where the Ordnung is repeated aloud to remind church members of all the rules. This service lasts about four hours.

Women

- The clothes must be made of dark colors, such as dark blue, green, gray, and black. The material shall be made of Dacron, broadcloth, rayon or polyester. The seams on the dress shall be narrow, no more than 5/8 of an inch wide. The pleats sewn in the back of the dress shall be no more than ¾ inch wide, and shall be ironed but not to the bottom of the dress. The dress length shall reach the shoe tops. The apron shall have a 5/8 inch tie strap around the top section and be four inches shorter than the dress. Three pleats shall be sewn to the bottom of the dress and shall not be narrower than ½ inch and no wider than a ¾ inch.

- The cape accompanying the dress shall be pinned in the center of the lower back by the apron strap. At that point it shall be a V and gradually brought out as it comes up over the shoulder. The cape shall be cut in two sections as it comes over the shoulder to make it fit better around the neck. The cape is only allowed to cover the edge of the shoulder. There is one pleat in the back of the middle of the cape and two small pleats on each side. The front of the cape is neatly folded and pinned down below the chest. Capes are made of black or white cloth.

- The bow in the bottom of the back of the kapp has to be a ½ inch wide. The ribbon of the kapp must be tied under the chin. Married women must wear white kapps all the time. Girls over fifteen-years-old, who are no longer going to school, also wear white kapps at home during the week.

- Socks must be either black or dark blue, cannot come above the knees nor be ankle socks, and have rubber/elastic sewn in the top of the socks.

- Shoes must be black with black laces. The sole cannot be solid or wedged type—it must have a small heel.

- Underwear must be homemade. No elastic is allowed in the underwear, it must close with buttons.

- The Ordinance also strictly regulates the bonnets. The shawls [cape] must be made of certain material, a particular length and be black.

- It is against the Ordinance to use a scissor or a razor on any part of the woman's body. Women are not allowed to cut their hair, shave their legs, or underarms. Nor are they allowed to use any type of birth control.

Men

- The pants and shirts must be of dark colors, the type of cloth is also regulated, and usually blue or black. Pants must have buttons across the front (no zippers allowed). Two small pleats are in the back of the pants. The belt on top of the pants must be 1¼ inch in width. Shirts are not allowed to have lay-down collars, and only two buttons in the front of the shirts.

- The vest must reach the pants, and use only hooks and eyes to close it. The jacket shall overlap a couple inches of the pants. It also closes with hooks and eyes, and no collar.

- The hat must be either a black felt or straw hat. The brim of the boy's hat is 3½ inches wide with a 5/8 inch wide band around the hat. Straw hats are worn only in the summer months and the felt hat in winter. Exception is for a teenager, who may wear a black felt hat every Sunday. The married men's hat brim must be four inches wide, with a 5/8 inch wide band around their hat. The Bishops and the Preachers' hat brims are 4½ inches wide. Men are allowed to wear any color of store bought gloves during the week.

- Men are allowed to smoke tobacco, such as cigars and pipes. They are not allowed to have fancy smoke pipes, just a regular pipe. Cigars must be regular size such as Swisher Sweets®. Cigarettes are against the Ordinance. Chewing tobacco, such as Mail Pouch® or Beechnut®, is permitted. Rubbing snuff or dipping Copenhagen® is against the Ordinance.

- Men may not wear underwear, or have any type of pajamas. Socks must be dark colors such as gray, blue, or black. Two-piece store bought long johns are acceptable, the elastic from the pants is removed and replaced with buttons. The top part of the pajamas also must be altered with two buttons placed in front of the shirt, the same way as the outside shirt.

- Hair must be at least one inch above the eyebrows on the forehead. One inch after each side of the eyebrows, stop and make a straight corner downwards, to ensure the ears are covered at all times. Then cut the hair in the front just below the earlobe and go straight back. The Ordinance letter clearly states that ears must be covered at all times and the haircut must be straight.

Parent and child relationship

- The Ordinance states that a husband and wife are to bring their children up according to the rules of the Church. The Ordinance states the woman's place is in the house cooking, cleaning, canning, making clothes, and helping her husband raise their children. The man's role is to financially provide for his family.

Husband and wife relationship

- The Ordinance on sex between married couples is as follows: It is against the Ordinance to have sex on fasting holidays (this includes January 6th – known as Olde Christmas), Good Friday, the Sunday between the Ordinance and the communion service in the spring and in the fall, and on Thanksgiving.

- On fasting days Church members are not permitted to eat breakfast. They are to spend the forenoon together with their family in their house reading the Scriptures. In the afternoon, after lunch has been served, they are allowed to go visit family or friends.

Farming and tools

- Hardware on the horse harnesses, such as buckles and other metal parts, cannot be nickel plated, if they are, they are painted black. The entire harness must be black.

- No chainsaw use. No driving of a tractor, bulldozer, riding lawn mower, push lawn mower that is motor operated, a motor vehicle of any kind, or operate any motor driven boat.

- No ownership of stationary motors to do thrashing, grind feed, run the sawmill, shop tools, or washing machine. The rest of the motors must start by pulling a rope or crank. No tools may be operated by air or electric.

Buggy regulations

- No type of battery lights on buggies, or drum brakes. No triangle on the back of the buggy indicating a slow moving vehicle. Two kerosene lanterns, with red reflectors, are allowed for nighttime use only. During the day, lanterns must be kept inside the buggy. The entire buggy must be black. The dashboard must be 17½ inches tall. The Ordnung requires a total of six feet of gray reflector tape on the back of the buggy: two feet along the top, one foot at the bottom, and two 16-inch pieces on each side. The seat back must be 7½ inches in height. The buggy length and width must meet their stiff guidelines. Horse reins and harness must be black. Wheels must be wood with a steel band around the perimeter.

Political activity

- It is against the Ordinance to press charges or to file a complaint against any of the members with the local legal system, no matter how serious the issue. It is also against the Ordinance to vote on political issues or positions of any kind.

Furniture and the home

- The furniture in the home is also regulated by rigid guidelines. According to the Ordinance Letter they must follow all the specific measurements. It has to be stained in a dark color. No fancy trim is allowed. It must look plain.

- According to the Ordinance Letter the inside house walls must be painted white. The Ordinance also specifies how wide your window facing or how wide your door casings can be, and what color they are allowed to paint them. In most of the Schwartzentruber Amish homes the woodwork downstairs is painted dark; the upstairs woodwork is painted any dark color. The Ordinance also states that they are only allowed to hang dark blue or black curtains over their windows.

- The Ordinance Letter only allows plain silverware. Members are supposed to buy all their dishes as plain as possible. A flower here or there on the plate is acceptable.

- The bed sheets, pillowcases and the comforter have to meet the Ordinance guidelines, white.

Church leadership & discipline

- The Bishop is the church leader and has final say. The two preachers in his church are his first servants who will take turns with the Bishop to preach. The Deacon is the Bishop's second servant, who will not preach in church but read German Scripture out of the New Testament.

- Should any complaint come against a member, the Bishop will send two of his servants to investigate, either two of his preachers or one preacher and the deacon. They will bring their findings to the Bishop and he will have the final say on what punishment should be applied to the member who has fallen in violation to the Ordinance. If the allegations against the member are serious enough, yet they do not have direct evidence to pass judgment, they hold preacher meetings until either the member confesses, or in some cases where they are confident that s/he is guilty then they will pass judgment whether or not she/he confesses to the violations.

- If the violation is serious, the member is given opportunity to excommunicate (in the bann) him/herself from church, meaning automatic shunning from the flock. This usually means they are excommunicated for two to four weeks should no other complaints come against them. Should they decide to fight the Bishop's ruling they will then take it up with the church. If the church agrees with the Bishop's findings, they will then be forcefully excommunicated from the church. The Bishop, Deacon and preachers will say in their Ordinance that the members are free to speak on these issues. (Most of the time it is unwise to go against the Bishop and his servants, as they are apt to find the member in violation of the Ordinance.)

E.
Glossary

I think Amish speak is graceful. I'm not a linguist but, I've heard the language called Dutch or German. Some say it's a mix of those two plus Swiss, calling it Deutsch. The former Amish I know call their language "Amish." Here are two interesting facts:

- Amish is an oral language. Children learn from hearing family members speak.
- There are various dialects. Depending on the area of our country, Amish have different accents just like non-Amish with northern or western roots. Think New Yorkers vs Midwesterners.

In 2013, I penned a blog post about their accent, which many try to hide. One former Amish told me he took speech lessons to conceal his accent. It's hard for them to completely erase their brogue. To me, their accent is endearing.

Below is a short glossary of Amish words. Some have different spellings because, being an oral language, there's no right way to spell them. Often a word is spelled phonetically. Ask an Amish or former Amish to help you with pronunciation.

My ex-Amish friends helped me with this wordlist:

- Dawdy (daudy or dawdi) = Grandpa
- Mommi (maumy) = Grandma
- Maam = Mom
- Daelt = Dad
- Gma (Gmay) = Church
- Maan = Husband
- Englischer = non-Amish

- Frau = Wife *or* woman
- Humli = Calf
- Gut = Good
- Lobe = Praise
- Kapp = Head covering
- Bann = Temporary shun
- Vee bisht du hight? = How are you today?
- Shay = Nice
- Hochzeit = German word for wedding, means "high times."
- Sex = Six (seriously!)
- Bahaef dich = Behave yourself
- Kotz = cat
- Shtup gucka = Stop staring
- Du bisht shay = You're pretty
- Ich liebe dich = I love you
- Kissy = Pillow
- Haush-dier = Home furnishings
- Buch = Book
- Kutza = Vomit
- Buss = Kiss
- Schup-kaech = Wheelbarrow
- Shnuck = Cute
- Liebe = Love
- Roth = Red
- Laufa = Walking
- Dawdi Haus = Home on the family farm for grandparents to live.
- Vee gehts = How's it going?
- Eple Saas = Apple Sauce
- Maidals = Single gals
- Sei Still (schtill) = Be quiet